CSU Poetry Series XXXVI

ALIVE ALL DAY

Richard Jackson

Cleveland State University Poetry Center

ACKNOWLEDGMENTS

Black Warrior Review: "The Other Day"
College English: "The Italian Phrase Book"
Crazyhorse: "Shadows," "A Violation"
The Gamut: "True or False"
Georgia Review: "The Head of the Devil"
Indiana Review: "The Angels of 1912 and 1972"
Laurel Review: "History"
Mississippi Review: "Self Portrait of Rivard By Jackson," "Victor Hugo's
    Hunchback of Notre Dame By Richard Jackson"
Missouri Review: "Who We Are, and Where"
Nebraska Review: "My Cruelest Muse"
New England Review/Bread Loaf Quarterly: "While Dancing at the V.F.W."
North American Review: "The Sum of the Drafts Exceeds the Whole"
Passages North: "Homeric," "Letter From the Outdoor Cafe"
Ploughshares: "The Dogs of Dachau," "For a Long Time I Have Wanted to
    Write a Happy Poem"
Poetry: "Eight Ball"
Prairie Schooner: "Hope"
South Florida Poetry Review: "Acknowledgments"
Tar River Poetry: "The Yellow Light of Begunje"

"Shadows" won the 1989 Crazyhorse award and appears in *The Best of Crazyhorse* (U. of Arkansas Press, 1990). "The Head of the Devil" also appears in a limited edition of poems of place published in Italian and English by Gemelli Press (1992). "A Violation," "Homeric," and "The Angels of 1912 and 1972" appear in the anthology *New American Poets of the Nineties* (Godine, 1991). "The Angels of 1912 and 1972" and "The Sum of the Drafts Exceeds the Whole" appear also in an anthology, *Poems From the Merrimack Valley* (Lowell, 1992).

I wish to thank the Fulbright Foundation for a grant as exchange poet to Yugoslavia, the Slovene Writers' Union for its hospitality on several visits, as well as the organizers of the Sarajevo Poetry Days Festival, the Belgrade Writers' Union, the Budapest Writers' Union, and the NEA for a fellowship which gave me some needed time.

Funded Through
Ohio Arts Council

727 East Main Street
Columbus, Ohio 43205-1796
(614) 466-2613

For Marg

CONTENTS

. . . Dear girl,
this: that we loved, inside us, not One who would someday appear, but
seething multitudes; not just a single child,
but also the fathers lying in our depths
like fallen mountains; also the dried-up riverbeds
of ancient mothers—; also the whole
soundless landscape under the clouded or clear
sky of its destiny—: all this, my dear, preceded you.

—Rilke, *The Third Elegy*
Trans. Stephen Mitchell

For no reason other than an oxcart these things
may happen. For blameless degrees of horses and wildcats. For no
reason but that your name is your name, and some did and didn't
remember it. For no reason other than zebras didn't have stripes.

—Edwin Rivera

I

A story tells a truth or a lie—is a wish, or a truth,
or a wish modified by a truth.

—Randall Jarrell

This evening won't let me be, it's a toy,
and I am a child who just has to take it apart
and put it together again, or else
the curiosity will drive me wild
and the emptiness blind me with its sad song.

—Edvard Kocbek

THE ITALIAN PHRASE BOOK

Good morning. Good afternoon. Good evening.
My name is Richard. Here is my passport.
I have nothing to declare. Even before you see them,
you can smell the first stars over the ancient arena.
There is a message for you of the greatest urgency.
Across the Piazza Bra the light escapes from a window
as though it were confessing its fears. Another
forced march begins in the lost provinces of the heart.
Where is the nearest taxi stand? the nearest telephone?
To the right. To the left. Straight ahead.
You can walk there. You can take the bus.
Someone is missing. Word of him can be heard
where the cricket songs are igniting the grass,
where even the streetlights tremble in the fog,
where even the thorns threaten the wind.
Please consult your phrasebook for the proper response.
Two blocks on the left. Turn right. Do you have anything
I want? How much will this cost? Will you have something
to drink? You can point to the proper question or answer.
What do you know about the early martyrs
who wavered before the lions in this arena,
who wept, ashamed, into their own arms? You do
not have to know the exact words. The wind from some
far place does not have to fill your shoes. The theater
where Catullus played is on the other side of the Adige.
He would sit there each night, more alone than the invisible
stars. One moment, please. Wait. Hold on. We cannot
answer everything. What could we tell you about the years
Dante spent exiled here from Florence? For him it was
all assassins, and the heart's gravediggers who abandoned
their half completed holes to the dark. For him it was
the moon dripping in the fields outside the walls.
Down this street is the supposed tomb of Juliet. The lovers

have dropped their notes in languages we might translate
through other books in this series. This is a good time
to practice ordering wine for the two of you.
We suggest the local Soave or Pinot Grigio while you wait.
Across the piazza a violinist is playing for coins,
playing as if to cover the cough of the moon,
as if he were tending the wound of some distant star.
This is a good time to toast your love. You may mention
the uncut meadow, the haystacks waiting to take shape,
how all the roads to the past have been closed,
how each night she tightens around you with the dark.
Down this street, the Piazza Erbe with its famous umbrellas
and market. You will find fresh peaches and pears.
You will find fresh oranges. Here you will be able
to practice many phrases. Be careful about numbers.
Nearby is Juliet's balcony. There are streetcorners,
whole towns not shown on your map. There are the dead
who still lean against the buildings without the proper facts.
There is Love crouched beside the stalled car on a side street.
Without practice, all your new phrases will evaporate
from the city streets like rain water. Don't worry.
Here is a night's growth of fog, covering the fountains,
disguising the few tourists who are still out, like you.
Here comes night wrapped in a shadow of remembered scents,
stopping at your table, opening her sack for you.
What is this made of? Can we agree on a lower price?
Using these idioms you will soon sound like a real native.
Can you help me find what I want? How far is it?
In the Gobi desert scientists have unearthed an 80 million
year old lizard never before known to man.
Beneath the market they have found an Etruscan village.
Would you care for another glass of Pinot Grigio?
It is said in today's paper that all news of our universe
travels the crest of nearly imperceptible gravitational waves
which we can decipher only months later. It was in this square
that the Roman priests would read the entrails of strange birds.
So it seems that only later will today's news reach you.
It seems the phrases are filling with desert and salt.

It seems the crows have been unspooling across the Piazza Bra
for an hour, the very hour your friend has turned his car
into the wrong lane half a world away. What is the tense for this?
What is the proper word? Please listen, then repeat the following:
I feel sick. I would like to see a doctor. I am only a tourist here.
I have this ear ache. I have a terrible headache. I have a toothache.
I feel nauseated. It hurts here. It hurts here. Where is
the nearest pharmacy? When should I call again?
Our connection was cut off. It was a country road,
the other car coming through the fog over a hill.
Can you find your way alone? Will you need assistance?
It was late afternoon. He must have been reciting
his favorite Byron, his favorite Dante, turning their grief
into love, letting Death sing all the old love ballads
with his steel guitar, with his smoky notes. It is not possible.
I have this headache. How much will it cost?
It hurts here. Is this enough? Just a minute,
here comes despair picking up the used cigarette butts.
Here are the old poems crouched in door stoops.
If you cannot find the correct phrase
try combining elements from the ones you already know.
Even the sky is prepared to lie about its moods.
Each star, a footlocker of old dreams.
What is your shadow doing there, bent over against the wall?
Please consult the phrase book for the proper response.
My love, whose fingers are matches, whose waist is
encircled by the arms of the wind. My love, how the world
sleeps in your throat, how your heart is filled
with the scents of raspberries and grapes,
to live inside you, to live inside the warm peach.
Otherwise there is no way to stop despair from lurking
all night in the shadows beside the old toll gate.
Otherwise we will have to weep in another language.
It was on a country road. It was in the wrong tense.
How do we stop all our words from falling in love with gravity?
Otherwise we will have to stop taking breaths
from this moment on. From this moment on
the abandoned clocks will observe us. My love,

our hearts are growing full of broken wings.
My love, to find our voice in a drop of water,
in the tracks the starlight leaves behind.
If only this were enough. If only we could get
the attention of Time, standing in that doorway
peeling an apple. It hurts here. It hurts here.

THE OTHER DAY

On the other hand, to no longer wish oneself
to be everything is to put everything into question.
—Georges Bataille

I just want to say a few words about the other
day, an ordinary day I happen to recall because
my daughter has just given me a yellow flower, a buttercup,
for no reason, though it was important that other day,
that ordinary one when the stones stayed just stones
and were not symbols for anything else, when the stars made
no effort to fill the spaces we see between them,
though maybe you remember it differently, a morning
when I woke to find my hand had flowered on the breast
of my wife, a day so ordinary I happened to notice
the old woman across the street, hips so large it is
useless to try to describe them, struggle off her sofa
to pull down the shade that has separated us ever since,
her room as lonely as Keats' room on the Piazza di Spagna
where there was hardly any space for words, where I snapped
a forbidden photo that later showed nothing of his shadow
making its way to a window above Bernini's fountain,
a shadow that hesitated as if to open one of Fanny Brawne's
letters before deciding to take them to the grave unread,
who knew how little his own death must mean to the boys playing
in the Piazza below, a shadow that I later understood as
my own, indecipherable, but I just wanted to tell you about
that other day, the ordinary one, when the drunk turned over
under the local papers beneath a bush in the park, when another
in a T-shirt, tatooed, picked up the paper to check
the lottery number, then put it down, secure it was
just another ordinary day, that happy day in which
nothing left my shadow, that sorrowful day in which
nothing entered, while I took my mother to the clinic at noon
to burn away the spot on her lungs not nearly as large
as the one Keats fought, walked along the river alone,
bought broccoli for my favorite soup, and good wine,
hummed a pitiful song unconsciously, on that day

when a few million cells in each living thing died
and were replaced perfectly, when I wrote a few words,
crossed them out, wrote others, that day, I can tell you
now, when someone left a bunch of yellow flowers, buttercups,
on the grave of a nameless child burned forty years ago
in a circus fire, leaving also the child's name, Sarah,
which is why I remember that other day, because it seems
if her story could be known thousands of other ordinary days
that belonged to her might also be known, and I could tell
my daughter why I have this sudden desire to weep
all day, why I weep for the names of the dead continuing,
Samir Sayah, 16, shot in the stomach by soldiers,
Amyad Nafea, 18, shot in the chest by soldiers the moment,
perhaps, my cat scratched the door, while the cicadas
began their afternoon thrumming on that ordinary day
where I found myself powerless and guilty once again,
a day so ordinary the descendents of the very lice that bothered
Christ began their work in the hair of the boy trying
to outrun the soldiers, an ordinary day, yes, when it was
not so impossible to go looking for the dead, though
I must say that of all the deaths that inhabit me
the one the other day was the least noticed lately,
so small that I imagined myself alive all day,
holding a yellow flower, just one, just to remember,
a day I can almost forget except for its likeness to today,
a day I must call ordinary because if it is not so
ordinary then Christ, we are pitiful for our poor laments,
the deaths so small we must imagine ourselves alive all day.

ABOUT THE DOGS OF DACHAU

I'd even given you part of my shared fear:
This personal responsibility
For a whole world's disease that is our nightmare.
                                        —Sidney Keyes

About the hearts of dusk that could make
pets of dogs the Nazis abandoned as they fled.
About turning to answer the dust devil
scuffed up by the wind, thinking I heard your voice,
and seeing the Rottweiler rise, alarmed, from the gravel.
About the Shepherd out near the disinfecting shack
nosing decades-old scents along the inner fence.
Also, about Mr. Valincourt's Doberman,
another summer, 1956, the olive
drab coat I borrowed from my father
caught on the chain link fence where I played army.
About that lost world where I carried death
on my shoulders, where the moss on the moonlight
said nothing yet about the piles of dead shoes.
Nothing of what I want to tell you.
About the dogs clamoring at the sound of a distant train,
about the shell casings of words we wanted to forget.
About this place.
About the fragment of a mouth organ
I found along the stream that is
still crossed by barbed wire. About the way
it freezes in winter and the man caught on the wires,
1941, the museum photograph says,
a spider's pod of snow wrapping around him.
About this place.
About our love in a world where the air is swollen,
where clouds only bruise the sky,
where stars refuse to connect as constellations.
About the coats heaped in a pile at one end of the camp.
About the lice, so many they could move an empty arm,
as if each coat were alive.
About those coats you can still hear

on a camp bench, maybe looking over a makeshift
chessboard and through themselves at the tourists.
About how clean this place is. The past
trying to stay only in the past. About the unbelievable
postcards, showing collections of rings,
hair, teeth, the body's trash dump.
Why I sent you the blank card from here.
Why my terror went looking for clothes,
poking like a searchlight through rags of words.
Why I wanted to hold you until we turned into birds
because here it is only the birds that are not branded by fire,
because they can turn into specks, then stars
so distant we can never disturb their light.
About the swamp at one end of the camp,
and the town at the other where the smell must have drifted.
About no one wondering. About the cries of the dogs
interrupting the still nights in that town.
About the old questions darkening the trees of the town,
and about the old answers lighting the tree tops.
About these sentences that cannot stop
at the horizon. These words with their nervous jugulars.
About everything returning, as Nietzsche threatened it would,
the pack of shadows crossing the yard like dogs,
the one turning to snarl like Mr. Valincourt's Doberman
at the coats who must stand for hours in the yard nearly naked,
at the execution procession with its slumped coats
stumbling through the mud, forced to play
the grotesque violins and trombones for their own deaths.
About this mouth organ, if that's what it is,
the rust and wood crumbling like a badly remembered song.
About how the inmates put on the night, the day,
how they put on tomorrow, the erratic flight of a butterfly
that has escaped the snapping dogs,
put on even the flowers, the trees, the windows,
how they put on the camp weather vane
which is another name for the soul.
About this tabloid I bought pointing to the frog boy,
kept alive by authorities like a huge tadpole,

peering out from his home in Peru.
About the huge coat he tries to hide in like a pod.
About wanting to kiss those eyes
bulging from his forehead, the flipper arm
reaching out as if to brush a fly. About the dogs, the town dogs
that go crazy when he is wheeled out to the yard.
About the dogs of Dachau,
how they sleep beneath the barracks like pools
of water that do not reflect the sky,
how their cries stiffen the coats and rub the eyes of morning.
About one of these coats, Esad. About the way
he slumps in his bunk, peering out like the frog boy,
the dysentery leaking from the bunks above.
About his festering foot sticking to the straw.
His experimental foot observed by the camp doctor.
About how even the starlight shakes the wind
carrying the screams from high altitude experiments,
cold water experiments, malaria experiments,
and how the echoes of the dogs sniff through
the abandoned ghettos of the heart.
About the woman. The way, each night,
he would tremble before her in his own skin
like a cyprus whose sparrows are
stirring to leave. About skin,
about flesh, because it is so alive taking flight.
About the way he dreams us, the way the coats
in those camp photos dream someone will wonder,
decades later, who they were. About his dream of
the way I rise from you, slump to the side like he does,
and the way you cry, the way we both cry maybe
just because we can make the stars into constellations,
because we have skin to touch and to cover.
About the simple coats we put on, putting on the world.
About this small mouth organ he must have refused to play,
a few keys tuned too high at one end for the dogs.
About fashioning it out of splinters from the bunks,
of metal from the camp shop, of the sky
that shrugged above his childhood in Istria,

the broken wings he fixed, the pain
of the quarter moon afraid it couldn't go on.
About the pockets it was carried in, the old faces
that crowd onto it like a sinking boat,
to snap it against the palms of our words,
so that the leaf will not have to face its death alone,
so that the whole landscape will turn into music,
this small mouth organ, this graveyard of voices,
from which no song must ever be finished.

THE HEAD OF THE DEVIL

Whoever this did not happen to,
whoever escaped wearing the long overcoat of sadness at the end,
who could watch the morning light fatten itself on the campfires,
on the neon lights outside the distant cafe,
just be thankful it wasn't you.
There is no sense trying to stop the wind from
caressing the switchblade branches.
There is no sense trying to cut away your own shadow.
It is erasing the road made by your shoes.
It personifies each secret you wanted to forget.
But there is no sense trying to forget the world
the way the monk Savonarola did four centuries ago,
warning about apocalypse and making images for hell.
Whoever you are, just be thankful it wasn't you.
It was here in Florence that Dante knew the horizon
of wolves around him. It was from here he was banned
for having the wrong map on his tongue.
Even then all the rumors were marked with tiny construction flags.
There is no sense trying to explain why they had turned, too,
on their leader, Savonarola, and burned him in this piazza.
After his death, a plague of caterpillars
devoured the sloe bushes for miles around.
Their human faces were marked with crosses.
Some said they had the head of the devil.
You can see that face even now in the gargoyles of the churches.
This is something officials everywhere deny.
Those are the ones who build the stone mouths
to receive whatever secrets one citizen tells about another.
So there's no sense trying to believe the traitorous heart will not
pull the lever on the scaffold of desire,
or asking if the leaves could find their way back to the branches.
There is no sense trying to forget. Just be thankful.
Just be thankful it wasn't you
when the stray bullet arrived for Rayvon Jamison,
nine months old, while he was standing in his crib in New York.

That was about the same time Voyager 2
found the 18th moon of Saturn buried
in one of its rings and the rival soldiers killed
600 refugees in the Lutheran Church in Monrovia, Liberia.
I mention these because whoever you are,
there is no sense trying to escape this world.
In poems we might make mermaids from sea lions,
we might compare fleeing warriors to sheep before wolves.
We might call these night birds the fish of the air.
Or we might, like the great Tuscan painter,
show St. John leaving our world for the wilderness,
show him as he dwarfs the town he turns his back on.
Even the great Leonardo wanted to ignore
the evidence he found that denied the biblical flood,
the sea shells buried in this valley, not on surrounding hills.
He, too, was afraid he had seen the head of the devil.
There's no sense trying to escape this world.
Maybe that is why he left his *Adoration of the Magi* unfinished,
the contour lines dissolving like salt lines at low tide
so that each figure seems to pass into the others around it.
In art, be thankful you can make a mountain waver in a breeze.
Just be thankful you can rejoice in the hidden desire of the rain.
Whoever you are, just be thankful you are still alive.
Just be thankful it is not your despair that must go
looking for its clothes in the city dump.
In the end, Savonarola's caterpillar produced no winged thing
and disappeared. Soon the common caterpillars flourished again
and soon the air was filled with their bright dance.
This was about the time they were burning scientists as well as poets.
They were hiding in their hearts a vague astronomy of hung men.
The truth trembled in the thicket like a wounded bird,
so it is appropriate here to mention Ramsey's mathematical model:
if we keep adding lines we will reach the point
where some pattern will occur, though it is a number
too big to calculate. For my part, I have my doubts.
There's no sense explaining to the deer
that it is the face of the mountain lion reflected in the water.
On one hand, it is good that there are constellations to guide us.

On the other hand it is good that there are extra stars.
They may be, as Savonarola said, the grace marks of God.
I am just thankful now when the flower opens
one time with the sun, without its usual complaint.
I am thankful for the spider who weaves across my door
each night, and I might as well mention my cat
who complains each morning how I am late to feed him.
There is no sense trying to escape the world.
Just be thankful, I tell myself.
Just be thankful, I would tell Savonarola
as he wavers on the scaffold, for that last pouch of breath
hiding out in your lungs. And whoever would ask the wind to rest,
whoever demands the moon lift its muzzle,
just be thankful you can
turn stones into clouds, into stars,
turn stars into frozen sparks, that you can
hold the world so close.
And whoever has seen the devil's head,
just be thankful you are still alive.
I can hear your heart beating in mine.

HOPE

I am going to talk about hope.
—César Vallejo

. . . fogged in with hope.
—Paul Celan

When I give the few dinars to the little pharaohs,
if we call these two gypsies by their right name,
when the boy tries to pull his sister away so that she
stares wide eyed at me, I cannot help thinking of
those photos of the poor gypsies the Nazis hung in the hills
just east of here. I imagine a young man, maybe
the grandfather of these two who has been directing them
from a few yards away, I imagine him hiding with the Partisans
in Marjin Pass, fingering by candlelight the worn
letter from his son. He must see in the steam that rises
from the winter's thin stew, by the light of a shot up
moon, a scene where some future daughter of his son is
playing Chopin on her piano, where the boy is kicking
a soccer ball against the side of a school, anything
but this scene which includes me, far from home, dreaming
the way he must have, wondering what has become of you.

You were right. The world slows down when you begin
to dream. Maybe it stops. The old pharaoh is
sitting on the 600 year old bridge of abandoned hope
in Mostar, abandoned by the architect a few days before
he finished it, who was found weeping beside the grave
he would enter if it fell. He is sitting the way my father would,
flicking cigarettes the way he did, Chesterfields, without
moving his arm, *how did he do that*, I'd want to know,
into the Merrimack river in Lawrence, Mass. They were stars,
he'd say, or candles, dying to make the dusk a little
brighter, that we retrieve whenever we borrow
a little light against despair. Listen, I am borrowing
that light. I am watching my two pharaohs working
the street, how the boy keeps tugging at her dress to make
her look more desperate. I am looking beyond them,

24

towards the grave of the poet whose name I can't pronounce,
who fought for the poor. I am lighting this candle for him.
And I am looking towards our poet, towards César Vallejo—
"Down the road my heart is walking on foot,"
he wrote, the poet who never lived where he was,
who knew, years before, how he'd die in Paris in the rain.
I see him as a child no older than these pharaohs, in Santiago
de Chuco, Peru, four days by horseback to the nearest
railbed, another day to the coast. One evening, he watches
a peasant being beaten for a few pesos, for a few words,
and knows, too, the future exile who will wander inside him.

Maybe it is impossible to live in one moment at a time.
Maybe Vallejo was right, that every moment we have is
a past we make into a future, or a future we must bless.
So maybe it is later, in another tense, in Sarajevo,
where you were startled for a moment by an old dream,
how the courtyard of the Serbian church became a hillside,
how as a child you used to dream of enormous animals
filling the windows. I think each dream is a hope we have
that we are not where we are. Each dream, my father
would say, is a dream of travel. Once by the Merrimack
we found the empty shells of beetles, dozens of them,
and he explained how they had been abandoned by horsehair
worms that grew three feet in their bellies, spiralling
like DNA until, almost becoming beetles themselves,
they abandoned one dream for another. To know anything,
he said, even love, is to know what lives inside it,
to know how we live inside each other, the terror
of any love. I did not understand that until this morning,
reading how Celan's poems grew smaller and smaller,
how he was afraid to talk directly because he feared
the Nazis were still listening, how his poems were codes
against despair. Certainly the pharaohs know that. I have
not forgotten these two, working their way back through
the crowd, handing the few coins to the grandfather,
handing over the years, the lives any moment holds.

I am handing this over to you, a little candle for the dark.
I am imagining the little pharaoh at her piano after all,
playing Chopin as her grandfather dreamed, I am thinking
of Chopin, beginning the second piano concerto, how
the piano seems to wait, awed by the orchestra's beauty,
or how the orchestra itself holds off what it knows will be
the plaintive entrance of the piano, how each gesture includes
the other. It was Chopin, like Vallejo, who would die
in Paris, in the rain, who was buried with a fistful of Polish
dirt, to stop, he hoped, his soul from wandering.

I am handing this over to you, a story for another time.
I no longer care what tense it is, what places we are
speaking from. What is any story but a form of hope?
Think even of the story of Osip Mandelstam, exiled
twice, tortured, how he asked in his last days only for
some candles and blankets. In one version he is thrown
out of the barracks by the other prisoners when he eats
their food, fearing the guards have poisoned his. His eyes
sink even deeper into his face than those haunting photos
of his early years, than the photos of gypsies, than the eyes
of my little pharaohs. He is living near the camp refuse heap
as winter approaches, the long gray beard beginning
to stiffen with sorrow, the gypsy of Vladivostok, still
making the hopeful poems he says only to himself.
One day he will look out to see *mounds of human heads*
wandering into the distance, and then himself out there,
dwindling among them, unseen, but perhaps rising again
from the dead, from his own poems, to see the sun starting.
He is hoping to find out what it means to live. He is
dreaming of sleighs, the shy currents of boyhood streams,
knowing how the earth is always ready to take him back.

By now the little pharaohs have crossed over the bridge
of abandoned hope and have dissolved like Mandelstam into night.
They have dissolved like Vallejo who tried to love everyone,
whoever is crying for death, whoever is crying for water,
who would die, as he knew, from a pain that came from

everywhere that Good Friday, 1938, the way the world was.
I would make them appear again, maybe later, maybe Belgrade,
in the faces of the pharaohs who will run beside us, selling
flowers, jewelry, anything, in a city the Nazis tried
to steal. They will never be the pharaohs of Egypt though
they keep their secrets as closed as the hidden chambers
of pyramids. I am thinking of the small cave, the small room
outside the Church of St. Peter in Belgrade, of how I stood
beside my friend as he lit the candles for his parents, *one
for death*, placing it in the sand on the floor, *but two for life*,
he says, two hanging in the urn in the middle of the air,
between earth and sky, past and future, a candle for hope.

There are no pharaohs much later where I am sitting
in the cafe in Slovenia with a poet who is telling me
over the weakening table candle in its green, gaudy cup,
how as a child he would wander the alps, how he could
name every bird, every tree, every thing that moved,
but now his voice breaks, he lights another cigarette,
another star, and he is telling me how he watched
the Germans pull his father from the house and shoot him
there in the street, how for years he felt, as Celan did,
that he had already died, that there was no word for hope.
We could be still sitting there, trying to separate the words
we have for fear and for hope. We could still be sitting there,
trying to find the secret codes Celan used in his poems,
even the bleakest, words that meant *we are still alive.*

Look, this is a moment that is not going to stop entering
your future, the way the boats of pharaohs were meant
to carry their dreams to whatever future the god had hoped,
beyond their deaths, beyond their suffering, gathering all
time around them,—as here in Mostar, Belgrade, Slovenia,—
as here in Venice where we will walk past Byron's mansion
near the old post office, where, when Teresa Guiccioli left,
he imagined her everywhere, sitting in the plush chair
in the corner, at the table with wine, along the canals.
I am standing there now. I am lighting a candle again

in the Church of St. Mark's for my little pharaohs, for Vallejo,
the gypsy poet who would walk brooding alone for hours,
for Mandelstam, who could find hope in the garbage of a prison
camp, for the sweet music of Chopin, I am lighting it
for all of us, handing it over to the memory of Celan,
and handing it over equally to the future of Celan, and to you,
the poet of slow dreams, I am lighting this candle for you,
a little light against despair, a little blessing for love,
a candle for death, a candle for life, a candle for hope.

FOR A LONG TIME I HAVE WANTED
TO WRITE A HAPPY POEM

Between two worlds life hovers like a star.
—Byron

It is not so easy to live on the earth
as an angel, to imitate the insects that dance
around the moon, to return what air we borrow
every few seconds. I am going to enter
the hour when wind dreamt of a light dress
to stroke, when water dreamt of the lips it would meet.
The famous Pascalian worm will just have to find
another heart to eat.
I will reveal the actual reason birds fly off
so suddenly from telephone wires.
The road will ask my foot for help.
The lightning will forget its thunder.
I will discover the hidden planet
to account for Pluto's eccentric orbit.
Pluto, of course, is ready to leave the alliance.
No longer will I have to lament
the death of Mary, the circus elephant,
hung with chains from a derrick on Sept. 16, 1916,
in Erwin, Tennessee, to punish her immortal soul
for brushing her keeper to death.
She looks out from her daguerreotype
as if she knows one day we too will hear
the stars gnaw away at our darkness.
It is not so easy.
One day I will free the clouds frozen in ponds.
No longer will the wind lose its way.
I will start hearing important voices like a real saint.
The Emir of Kuwait will answer my call.
If I am not careful I will loosen
the noose of history from around my own neck.
Just to keep sane I will have to include my weight
which is the only thing that keeps me from being a bird.
Walking on air will no longer be a problem.

Meanwhile, the Hubble telescope is still wobbling
its pictures from outer space so we will
have to rely on imagination a little longer to see clearly.
Why don't windows tell us everything they see?
Here come the characters of my sad poems.
They have been standing in line to get in
like fans for a rock concert.
They are gathering around Beatrix Potter who spent 30 years
locked in her room. The maid brings up her supper.
She sneaks out into the garden to capture
small animals to draw or reinvent before they die.
Beatrix, I say, we no longer have to kill what we see.
I know this in my heart, in my wolf, in my owl.
In the Siena of my palms. The Bergamo of my head.
In the garlic of my fingers. My friends say
I use too much. There are never enough
streets crossing the one we are stuck on.
No one wants to be a cloud anymore.
Who still believes in the transmigration of souls?
If you believe Bell's theorem, then the fact is
that the squirrel falling out of my tree this morning
makes minute sub-atomic changes from here to Australia.
Will I have to put on my pants differently now?
Just when we start to believe in moonlight
we notice how many stars it erases. It is not easy.
I am going to come back
as the birthmark on the inside of your thigh,
between your dreams of angels and solar dust,
between your drunken skirt and the one that laughs.
I am going to learn what the butterfly knows
about disguise, what so astonishes the hills.
All this is going to take constant vigilance.
In *The Last Chance Saloon*, Tombstone, Arizona,
I saw the lizard creature with its glued head,
almost human, tilted up from under the glass,
as if it didn't know which world to claim.
Apparently it fooled a lot of people in 1872.
I kept thinking if only Ovid had seen this creature

he would have known his nymphs
could never escape just by turning into trees.
In Dora Noar, Afghanistan, the young soldier,
Mohammad Anwar, age 13, believes he will turn
into a desert flower when he dies in the jihad.
The barrel of his AK-47 is sawed down
because he is as small as the four prisoners
he has returned with. They understand
that all we know of the sky we learn by listening to roots.
I was happy, he says after shooting them
against a wall, over and over again, *I was happy.*
Happy. Now maybe the earth will want to change its name.
It won't want to be the earth anymore.
Shadows will be abandoned by their objects.
The light will squander itself on the flowers
because they do not even want to be flowers anymore.
It is not easy to live on this earth.
We don't understand that the universe is
blowing away from us like litter,
but at an incredible speed.
There is a new theory that the universe is left-handed.
It has to do with the spin of quarks.
Someone else says it's in the form of a horseshoe.
The rest of the animal is metamorphosed into a black hole.
I happen to side with the fanatics who believe
it is following the call of a mythic bird too distant to see,
but this is only poetry, like the old papers
the homeless use to stuff their clothes on cold nights,
the kind of poetry that says, flowers, be happy,
trees, raise your drooping eyebrows,
sky, don't turn your back on us again,
my love, how wonderful to have lived while you lived,
which is not the sort of poetry you read anyplace anymore.

NIGHT OF THE MOON LIKE A GUITAR

I'm a god, but not the oppressive kind.
I am responsible for blocking that thimble edge
of moon with my clumsy planet. But I don't
make any claims for the timetable of
the cosmos Spinoza described a while back.
My grandmother always packed a thimble
on the train from Methuen to Boston,
sewing the finger tips of my woolen gloves.
I loved the way they smelled, wet from snow
and drying over the radiator. Every time I touch you
I remember how smooth those gloves
made my skin. She made the best
fudge and panucchi and gave the recipe
to my father who forgot to give it to me.
I would give it to you if I knew it.
Each night I listen to the signatures
of constellations to decide what fugue
should control the way we spin.
Spinoza is just the little conductor asking
for your tickets, singing out your next stop.
Tonight the moon wants to be a guitar,
wants the shape of your ear, of that oblong
star, a red giant 200 million light years away.
Agreed, it's not very much to ask of anyone.
Whoever tunes themselves by moonlight
will be happy. Whoever fingers the moon
like a nickel will be rich. Whoever
eats its thin wafer will be saved.
Don't pull the dark horizon around you like a blanket.
Don't be afraid of the mysterious light
that has started to emanate
near the galaxy's center.
It pulsates like that train light approaching
the station to tell me my grandmother
would climb down in a few minutes

with the milkpail of sadness she stopped to pick
like berries in Reading or Wakefield that afternoon.
She would tell me the world is as old
as the time it takes for the heart
to turn exile, to forage
in the gulleys of songs we forget to sing.
Have you ever noticed how many people
think their sandals have wings?
Just listen to the moon's nocturne.
Two ice ages ago this was the same moon
that witnessed the last meal of a dinosaur
found recently in Ohio. The swamp grass
and lily pads were never digested. It was as if
he wandered off like a kid chasing a ball.
I could tell you something very similar
about the mummy behind the glass case
in Urbana. They haven't even determined its sex
because the owners don't want anyone to open it.
You might get a little DNA by scraping
the inside of the skull. But it seems
after thousands of years people are still
afraid to touch. I bet that's why no train wants
to pass through Urbana. Some people, like my friend,
Diana, hunt you down and shoot you full of arrows
as soon as you look at them the wrong way.
This almost happened to me in Venice when someone
asked me for directions and I turned, leaning,
touching his shoulder and pointing towards
our bleak future. The pilgrims at the door today
preached about the end of the world.
When I told them I was a kindly god
their hands dropped out of mine
like parachutists out of one of those transports
in a World War II movie. In *Dead Reckoning*
Humphrey Bogart is a paratrooper,
back on leave, whose friend
jumps off the train taking them to Washington
and a hero's welcome. Later, the friend

turns up dead and Bogart protects
the woman he knows is the real killer,
but whom he loves anyways: "Just tell it to me
with Christmas in your eyes and a low voice," he says.
Some days I'm not a god, just Humphrey Bogart.
I have a fedora in the shape of a spiral galaxy
I bought for 25 bucks. I have a field
whose stars are alive as fireflies.
You'd be surprised how often,
on its hike towards dawn, the sun gets lost.
I have always admired how bones, in times
of stress, try to escape the body. I love
your delicate wrists. I love the smell
of your hair. Isn't it astounding
that moths always seem to find us
in the night? The moon is leaping
from stone to stone to cross the creek.
It is trying to be wind. It is trying to be water.
That must be the 11:16 on the Amtrak line.
I have never liked it when all the clocks strike
at once. The dark stops at my door.
The sea remembers my steps.
Love is everything. Just ask
the moon that wants to be a guitar.
The empty branches are tuning themselves
by its light. And though the universe is
filled with cold dark matter no star will
ever reveal, there is no reason to be afraid.
Fear turns out to do the most damage
on our planet. When you turn in sleep
I brush the shadow of my fingers across you
as if it were that time when I stood
on the station steps trying to let my fingers
pick the cutting steel of my grandfather's
Martin 12 string, a guitar almost as big
as I was. John Lee Hooker. Lightning Hopkins.
Brownie McGhee. Bessie Smith.
I feel so lucky today just because

there's this audience of stars pasted
to the Vermont ceiling I've been sleeping under.
Because the crows are rising from the tracks
like eighth notes. Because the light
wrinkles on the sheets. But most of all,
because it is Wednesday,
the day after Tuesday, the day I reserve
for solving the heart's astronomy,
just this moment when one star dies
and another is born in that stellar nursery
called Sagittarius A, just at this
precise moment, or some other moment,
while the frets of the moon cover your skin
as if they were the shadows of blinds,
as we turn once again into each other, as you
open your sleepy-eyed breasts
that leave even the moon
speechless, that stop the lantern
from swinging in the hand of the signalman
and allow the tracks to finally converge at infinity,
which really doesn't mean much to anyone
unless, maybe, to the woman,
who must be Daphne, who must be Artemis,
who must be you, who slips into the pond at night,
caressed by the constellations it holds, bear, hunter,
scorpion, by the notes and half notes of the moon.

II

Who is wandering again near the porch
calling us by name?
Who has pressed his face against the icy glass of the window
and is waving his hand like a wind-blown branch? . . .
In response in the cobwebbed corner
a sunbeam dances in the mirror?

—Anna Akhmatova

THE ANGELS OF 1912 AND 1972

It is a long time since I flapped my wings,
a long time since I stood on the roof of my house
in Lawrence, Mass., or Michael's in No. Andover,
a little whiskey in one hand, the past slipping
through the other, a little closer to the heaven
of dreams, letting the autumn wind, or the spring
wind, or maybe just the invisible breath of some
woman lift me up. It is a long time since I have flown
like a swallow, or even the clumsy pigeon, into another
time, practicing miracles, dodging the branches
of lost dreams that cut against the sky,
and the rocks thrown by small boys, finding
the right nest under the eaves of some pastoral age
even the poets have forgotten, or fluttering
to a slow landing on some ledge above the buses
and simple walkers of this world. It is a long time.
From where we stood I could see the steeple of the French
church. Further back, it was 1912, and I could almost
see the tenements of the French women who worked
the fabric mills, weaving the huge bolts of cloth,
weaving the deadly dust into their lungs.
They could hardly fly, these angels. I could
almost see them arching down Essex street and
Canal street to the Everett mills, the Essex mills,
pushing against the police horses for two bitter years,
thousands of them, asking for bread and roses, asking
something for the body, something for the soul.
If I did not fly so far I could see my mother's father,
years later, stumble to the same mills, nothing gained.
Or I could have looked ahead to this very year, and seen
Bob Houston and me standing on a roof in Bisbee, Arizona,
two desert sparrows flying blind against the night
once again, remembering the union workers herded
into boxcars and shipped from there into the desert
a few years after my French weavers flew down

Essex street. But it was 1972 and we still believed
we could stop the war with a rose, as if there were
only one war and not the dozens of little ones
with their nameless corpses scattered like pine cones.
It was 1972 and we stood on the roof like two angels
lamenting the news that John Berryman had leaned out
over the Washington Avenue bridge in Minneapolis,
flapped his broken wings, dropped to the banks below him.
I am a nuisance, he wrote, unable to find a rose for his soul.
We thought we could stand on that roof in 1972, two
Mercuries waiting to deliver his message to another time.
I should have seen what would happen. I should have seen
my own friend on his bridge, or the woman who could have
descended from one of those French weavers leaning
on the railing of the north canal in Lawrence because
all hope had flown away, or my own father starting
to forget my name that same year. If there is anything
I remember now, it is the way he looked at me in his
last year, wondering who I was, leaning back against
his own crushed wings, just a few years after he told me
to fight the draft, to take flight, or maybe he leaned
as if there was a word no one would ever speak
but which he knew I would believe in, that single word
I have been trying to say ever since, that means
whatever dream we are headed towards, for these
were the angels of 1912 and 1972, the ones we still
live with today, and when you love them, these swallows,
these desert sparrows, when you remember the lost fathers,
the soldiers, when you remember the poets and weavers,
when you bring your own love, the bread, the roses,—this is flying.

WHILE DANCING AT THE V.F.W., SEDUCTIVE MELANCHOLY TAPS YOU ON THE SHOULDER

She's left a suitcase of dreams at the bus station.
She's left desire shivering without a coat on this chilly evening.
She's let the moon break free of its padlock.
All of a sudden a clandestine rustle of leaves.
In some far galaxy the abduction of a few important stars.
This is why she arrives as a premonition, one of those galactic
shock waves nudging us towards a future where we don't even exist.
You have to forget about applying obscure books of philosophy.
You have to be careful all the heart's pawns are not sacrificed.
In Slovenia she took the shape of Ismet who handed me
the photographs of children shot by the army in Kosovo.
He handed them to me the way a falling man
reaches for a handle or branch that isn't there.
It was a day the grass seemed to withdraw from the earth.
You have to take the photos, two brothers, Din and Asim,
aged eleven, who one morning dashed out from behind a wall
and were taken for rioters by the tank crew.
Sometimes it seems the stars are out only to protest
the darkness we make. The two boys squint
as if they were trying to find the boundaries of the wind.
Here at the V.F.W. no one has even heard of Kosovo.
An orchestra of silence is feathering its wings.
History is just a brass spitoon at the end of the bar.
Here is one old couple slumping into a pit of broken notes,
slow dancing, his knee searching the inside of her thigh.
Here is another eating his heart out of a box lunch.
They are all dancing like those painted figures on the bridge
at Lucerne, a dance of Death, the skeletons in the form
of soldiers, altar boys, beggars, even a priest
peeking out from a nun's bed.
They are dancing like meteors.
They are dancing like the lost neutrinos
everyone hopes will explain the origin of love.
This is about the time the red sky drops its curtain

with a lot of fanfare. Melancholy is there, making you
wonder for whom each star was intended.
This morning the past was poking among the trash cans
in an alley on 11th Street. This afternoon the phone message
seemed to come like one of those cosmic radio waves
from another age: *Warren has cancer all through him.*
It's in his brain. They can't find where it began.
You have to turn away. You have to remember how years ago
it was Warren who found the boy fallen forty feet from the ledge
still alive, broken, how Warren said it was good luck,
that we'd be immortal, that everything we touched
would be immortal. Is it one memory, or the way
each memory eclipses another that makes the soul so dark?
In a little while, any moment becomes like a canvas
ripped from its frame. Now all I can think of is how
we are made from atoms of long dead stars, how we never die.
It is lucky for us there is an unequal number
of quarks and anti-quarks or else they would cancel
themselves and us out altogether.
This is also true of Melancholy, walking the streets
and swinging her purse, and her clown of
a street cop, who in one of my dreams
goes under the name of history, who teases us
with the exact date when the number
of dead equals the number of living. You can see them
in the tabloids someone is reading on the next table.
They are pressing their noses against our windows.
The Oklahoma farmer who shot a 23 pound grasshopper.
The man in New York whose head was blown all over his spumoni
by a trick cigar. The East Indian guru who twisted his head off
6 years ago and never sleeps. Jim Morrison whose ghost is
cruising L.A. I myself have been seeing Ingrid Bergman
in several Northern Italian cities. So it is
no surprise scientists are going to blow up the moon
to stabilize life on earth. No tides. No wind.
This is why Melancholy and her clown dance the V.F.W.,
like those two stars revolving around each other
pulling their orbits into strange shapes Euclid would blush at.

I am watching the enormous man cover
his tiny partner like the huge funnel of a black hole.
I am trying the two-step myself, we are skipping
around the edge of the floor like two new comets.
You have to dream. You have to dance all night.
You have to realize the earth's magnetic field shifts
every few million years, and when it does it again
we will all be looking in the wrong direction.
This is why I still carry my father's G.I. compass.
This is why Warren and I would try to pocket a future
from a fruitstand on Haverhill street. Why the two brothers
in Kosovo open the back door of someone's sleep.
They are doing the dance of their native Albania.
You don't want to see them waltz off into
their own universe the way some distant stars have,
going so fast their light will never reach us.
Years later, Warren and I would be standing in a bar
like this, lamenting the deaths of our friends—by sniper,
by landmine, by friendly fire. The stars gather
like frost on the windows, and we are the only ones left alive.
We are riding one of those little wormholes in space
that take you from one time to another. For instance,
just recently I had a blood infection like the one
that nearly killed me thirty years ago. It was only in 1865
that Joseph Lister first used carbolic acid to disinfect wounds.
In the middle ages the Florentines catapulted dead donkeys
over the walls of Siena in the first instance of germ warfare.
All the angels there have already died into marble.
This is why I am surprised each morning when I wake alive.
Do you want to believe your own dream for the world?
In the turtles's dream, everyone flies. You have to
get down on your knees, tangled in the barbed
wire of history, facing the eternal tanks of the heart,
you have to learn the earth's dream for the flower,
you have to listen as the frog leaps onto the moon
while the rest of the lake is asleep, to hold each other
the way these dancers do, embracing even the stars
that are hidden by daylight, inventing a kind of gravity

scientists will never discover, you have to listen
for a friend's dying voice that is also the voice
of the egret singing against the contrary tides of the bay,
against whatever it is that would have you disappear.

HOMERIC

She just hauls out and smacks him
on the side of the head which sends him reeling
against the plate window of the Krystal
hamburger shop while the old couple inside,
she in the print dress, he in the light orange
polyester suit, just watch because they've seen this
a hundred times, maybe a thousand, and there's never
any reason to speak of, so that the boy just
straightens up, lowers his head, and walks
behind his mother. The old folks are there because
the Krystal hamburgers are steamed and soft
to their gums, and me because my new root canal
won't take too much pressure yet, and the mother
and son because there's not a hell of a lot to do in
Chattanooga, the Bible Belt, on a hot June morning, 1989.
There are a couple of choices: you can walk away,
letting the scene continue for generations and make, if you
know words, obscene art from someone else's pain;
you can abduct the kid in a dramatic rescue, which will
add to your pain and his; you can lecture the mother
in which case she'll take it out on the boy; or maybe
slap her silly, which is what I would have done
thirty years earlier, the year I discovered Homer's
rosy-fingered dawn, as preached by Sister Michael,
was really the bloody one Hector, Ajax and the others
made for themselves, and the one I knew then
on Lawrence and Haverhill Streets—the chains,
the black-taped flashlights, the kick boxers,
the knuckles, the whisper of zip guns—the year I had
enough of it from Charlie Pilch and his brother, and
so pushed them against the chain-link fence, amazed
as they were at how fast my fists were hitting them
until they fell bloody beneath me, no Homeric dawn,
no heroic fight, and then ran home to get sick
for my own stupid cruelty. I don't know how

I escaped that world where you were either lucky
or nearly dead, where we drank Hollihan's ale
behind the brewery when the night shift sold us
illegal, and we argued how we should have joined
the Hungarians throwing bottles of gasoline at Russian
tanks, not for nobility or freedom, but because that was
the way, how we should have dropped the bomb,
beat it out of any one who said we couldn't. I don't
know if the world I've entered is much better
because I'm clenching my fists inside my jeans,
biting so hard it's only my foolish and rootless
tooth that warns me back from the woman,
and I have looked over the rough idea of the world
this has become, the endless cars making their way
down Brainerd Road with their own gritted angers
to face, the polyester man snapping at his wife,
the hot sun which is just another star angry with itself,
the street preacher who's taken up his cross
with its bloodied spots for wrist and ankles, not
even him, none of them even noticing that boy
who has already walked off the world of poems,
who may or may not be lucky enough to escape
this or that world, drive his car, some used junk,
out to the levee or dam, look back over the city
lights that are okay even if they are not the tent lights
of the noble Greeks on the plains of Troy,
where he will remember from that safe distance,
like some Achilles still brooding over a small loss,
how his life, too, almost came to an end
on several occasions, some worth it, some not.

A VIOLATION

Whatever they said, those ten-foot lips pouting across
the screen at the Den Rock Park Drive-In, and they were
glistening with the light rain falling on some Balkan city,
my father was prepared to be earnestly embarrassed that night
he took three of us friends to see John Wayne in *Horse Soldiers*
and had to wait for this romance to be over. I was afraid we could
walk up to the screen like little cameras zooming in to see
the pores, the pimples, the ugly mole hair I had read Swift's
Gulliver describe, and which so violated my sense of romance.
But we were supposed to hate it, we were supposed to head
to the concession stand for cokes. Instead, we crouched
behind an old Rambler where we thought we wanted to be touched
by anyone, by the lovers silhouetted in those lips. It was
Arthur who snapped the picture with his pocket Brownie,
and it was Eddie who turned away for some pain we couldn't see,
not for the woman on the screen, though whatever love
or life she was pleading, she spent those last few frames
wandering the streets from one doorway to another
after refusing someone's love, until her life was lost among
the subliminal messages of the intermission ads. It would be
years before I thought of her again, in front of a perfect madonna
painted by Bellini, her small, sensual mouth bringing me back
to that same hopeless love, and once in front of a Balkan gypsy
I was photographing in a world I still thought was all romance.
It was romance I wanted us to be dreaming that night.
But it was two years before we learned the truth, how earlier
that summer Eddie had been found standing beneath a signal maple,
his jeans and underwear pulled down to his ankles, his tiny
sex bruised and red, his thighs raw from someone's switch—
he never said who—shivering probably as much as he did
that night at the drive-in we teased him to tears he couldn't stop.
I can't stop remembering him now. I remember this:
someone had taken pictures. Someone had left the yellow
film boxes scattered around his feet. He must have closed
his eyes. He must have stood there in his own dark, imagining

we would swarm over the ridge the way those horse soldiers might.
It was only today I remembered all this. I was standing
in a small church near Trieste where there still hangs a picture
of Mussolini peering from shadows the way Eddie's attacker must have,
peering at the shawled women who hobble up the aisle to the altar
to light a votive candle, to kiss the wounds, the feet of the crucifix,
trying to find forgiveness for the love they refused or denied,
il Duce violating their prayers, invading their dreams.
Everyone's, that is, except the photographer, blind since youth,
and his wife—except those two beside me, taking pictures,
he said, of our sounds, the hush of our shame, *the Mussolinis*
of each cruel act, he whispered, seeing not things but the echoes
between things, what they had been or what they might become,
our secret fears, our dreams of romance—that was it, he was
taking pictures of our dreams, more than we could ever imagine
at the Den Rock Drive-In, what with all our blown-up images
and that shattered life before us, Eddie Trainor, who in a few years
refused to see anything, trying to move his lips to speak,
motioning us away, the same motion that gypsy woman made,
a kind of madonna herself, trying to stop me from taking her
picture, her soul, and the souls of her two young children,
the girl hugging her thigh where they sat on the curbing, the boy,
Eddie's age, starting to work the evening tourist crowd,
for this too was a kind of rape, as so much has become—
what my father could not stop, holding Eddie in his arms,
for the love of life, he would cry, not knowing the story either,
the horse soldiers charging, the Mussolinis shouting, the madonna
weeping, her lips moving, her lips closing, the shutter not quitting.

THE YELLOW LIGHT OF BEGUNJE

I had time eating out of my hand
until Tomaz told me I was leaning on the German pillbox.
Then hope edged out onto a precarious branch.
Tomaz himself was turning in a circle
letting the yellow pollen fall all over him,
listening to the wail of a woman who made a ribbon of despair
from her dress before she faced the firing squad.
The history of the universe is tied together by these superstrings
of energy scientists have recently begun to unravel.
For example, at 3 a.m., August 7, 1943, at the residence
of Tomaz Salamun, a leaf fell from the oak tree
while here one of the ten Slovenes the Germans would kill
for each of their own the partisans had ambushed
slumped against the wall in the courtyard.
In 1988 we had just seen Metka's beautiful stained glass windows
in a church a few towns over, Easter Sunday,
the light collecting and tumbling above the worshippers
like wood chips at a saw mill. I was leaning against
the snide voice of some guard who let some partisan
run nearly to the trees before freezing him in the crosshairs.
Marg and Amy were listening with Laura to the old or crazy voices
that never bloomed, that were walking the narrow furrows
of light in the state hospital, nodding here and there
to the voices who were smoking a few evening cigarettes.
They were walking the way my father did,
and his mother before him when their memories turned weightless,
when all they could hear was the choir of planets,
when their hearts took the pure shapes of birds.
The lost years were not going to come out of their burrows.
In a little while we would sneak away along the drainage ditch
before it became too dark to see where we stepped.
I could still feel my father's captured luger
heavy as a dying planet in my hands.
Why was that night sky so black?
It may have to do with the red shift

which makes the huge number of receding stars invisible.
It may be that some light hasn't reached us,
that some other light died out and is imprisoned
by the stored-up energy in fruit and minerals.
It may have to do with certain shadows disloyal to the day.
It may have to do with the way one of the inmates, Milenko,
would never sketch the sun or stars on these slab walls.
It was a time when joy went poking in the garbage for a dream.
Each night agony walked down the prison corridor
to look in on one of her children.
The few words they remembered were all springing leaks.
Sorrow scampered into the corners beneath a few farms.
The vines of Milenko's scratched poems still break through
the mentions of lovers, flowers, sweat, dung, hope,
of how the stars must be germinating somewhere in the earth,
how his love had arms of wheat, eyes like nests.
On the back of one window slat he carved the eyes
that look beyond those of the SS officer who opens it
each morning. We were all trying, Tomaz,
Metka, Marg, Amy, Laura, trying to leave
our own voices there among those wandering voices.
Even now we want to peel the guilt from our skin like fruit.
Even now we are all under the spell of those superstrings
leading us to a day that is still waiting
around some corner like an assassin with a twitch in his eye.
For instance, somewhere inside me the faulty gene
of my grandmother and father will trigger certain
protein abnormalities, and I will begin to forget
the terrible light of the moon buried beneath these hills,
the whispers dropping like pollen from the branches,
Tomaz, Marg, everyone, even Milenko
who maybe now takes off the warm suit of his fever,
maybe now tries to saddle his runaway dreams.
He is not ready to believe in a sky that stables its stars.
He is not ready to believe he will not see the shadow
of the bullet approaching. What power does he think
might keep his stars from dying?
According to Blake, there are only two: love and hate.

For example, there is the guard eating candies
from a tin box painted with a place Milenko imagined each night.
There are also our lives swaying like these yellow daffodils.
They are swaying on some battlefield where two opposing
forces muster the atoms of hate in each of us.
Parmenides first recorded that the evening star is
also the morning star, Venus, appearing or fading.
The hearts on the walls of Begunje smolder faintly.
If only we could remember back to the first
fistful of matter the universe began with.
Every few minutes the searchlights orbit the fields.
However, the most accurate way to tell time is by proton decay.
The night is once again pulling on its polished boots,
once again ready to march against our horizons.
I have begun to lose sight of Tomaz and the others,
and of you, Milenko, who, it seems, thinks the morning star is
the bell his mother used to ring, not the rifle's shot.
You do not even hear the birds which have already become
bored at the way we repeat these ancient forms of torture.
You are no longer thinking about time which means how often
the first fusillade fails to kill the prisoner. You are no longer
waiting for a time when the birds will fly again
with our names on their wings. Each day our hearts
wander out of the rifle's range only to get lost in the woods
that slope gently into the foothills. Each day
spreads its black wings and settles above our heads.
This is why the universe will begin to cool and contract.
A few red dwarfs, a few cells in the brain, burning out.
A few soldiers waiting in ambush for the night to lose its way.
This is why all the homeless stars. Why the stained glass of memory.
Why the wind dies in the cup of the flower.
Why the breath conspires with the scarecrow of the new day.
Why the yellow light of Begunje refuses to bloom.

WHO WE ARE, AND WHERE

I think it was just as I was about to write you
how I found the old bent nail in my father's coat
that I knew you would suspect this might be another story
that holds within it someone's death, so I decided
to begin instead with the story of Bullwinkle,
not the cartoon character we both probably watched
on Saturday mornings, but the confused moose from upstate
Vermont who fell in love a few months ago
with Jessica, the Hereford Cow, insuring, by his clumsy
presence in the pasture, that she would have first place
at the hay bales and feed. There is a picture of Bullwinkle
nuzzling his head on Jessica's ample rump
while she looks wild-eyed and bewildered at the camera.
Later, as winter set in, he lost his antlers, as all
bull moose do, and so also the greater part of his libido.

In town, the talk is all about the moose position, and I can
imagine the jokes you would make, but I'm wondering
what chances the lovers might have next year. I've been
thinking of all this a few days after you left when everything
seems out of place. Do you remember the story of Louis
Castrano, the unlucky fisherman until thirty-four
largemouth bass fell at his feet out of a Fort Worth sky?—
carried by a high-altitude twister, some meteorologist reported.
Everything, you said, love, solitude, trust, hope,
is only an accident of location. I think you would say
the confused young moose won't return, that nothing is
ever connected. It's all a film, you'd say, where the words
of subtitles keep only a vague link to what is happening
on the screen—the Japanese villager, say, trying to explain
the mysterious green lights beneath his fishing nets in one
of those films meant to protest by a common code the chance
and monstrous effects of the bomb. You would say
I should remember Cesar Pavese, whose book you left,
and who found in the end that all his life was chance,

that the only thing left was the absurd vice of the body.
What I wanted to say was simple: this afternoon,
in a remaindered book stall I found Russ Vliet's novel,
Scorpio Rising, and remembered how he described the spring
quail eating the yellow berries of the agarite bush
by the roadside, darting out of sight of the cars,
to explain how suddenly his cancer came to bud,
and how silently it was burned away. It would bloom again,
we'd hear later, far from the dry riverbeds of South Texas
he would always seem to inhabit, like one of his own
characters returning to face the sky that seemed too white,
the skin of dust collecting on still pools for years.
"Thunder ain't rain," he'd say, "So you go on writing."
I'm trying to understand how in such a short while we are
only the few stories, the words someone remembers—
a lover, if we're lucky, and then silence, not even the sounds
of another language.
                    Not long ago I lay in another language
in a small boat at Golubac, a place that still means,
after centuries, "a dove," peace. I lay beneath the ruins
of the castle where the current forgets, where dawn
began to surface through the small circles the fish
gave us instead of themselves. The towers, the parapets
would give a stone to the Danube every few years,
falling past the graves, past the inscriptions
the Romans and Turks abandoned and where sometimes
the young lovers would hide out, or sometimes follow
a stone into the river. I never thought a place so lovely
could stand so long. I drifted on the river all day,
the hills around me as stark as those in South Texas,
listening to a procession of priests and faithful singing
their way into a church that may have stood beyond the hill,
my line weighted by that old bent nail, weighted
by all the stories of poets that say the place
we're in is never enough. As you hear that, you will know,
too, that I dreamt of you, that I remembered how we
discovered the poems of Dino Campagna the night you left,
poems that turned, at one point or another, into the same

woman or place. This was the place where Serbs and Turks
lost their nameless troops in another attempt to
discover whose light of God would spill across the cliffs.
This was the place where no one remembered, but were
themselves memories drifting down with the current.
This was a land, like Russ Vliet's, that inhabited you forever.

I think if I stayed long enough I could have outlived death.
A few days ago, in Boston, the derelict story teller,
John Griffin, who lived beneath the plywood lean-to
beside the "L" Street bath house when he was in town,
surely did. When they found his body twenty feet
from the water, half way, a little snow and sand
blown against his ribs, his clothes were burned off
and the broken sterno can was already cold in his shelter.
As you can guess, everyone has a story that includes him,
or tells the old war stories he told. Maybe we should
remember what Pavese knew, that what we should feel
confronting the dead is the terrible humiliation of our being,
as if we should apologize for our own frailty and fear.

Maybe that is why we are always trying to begin again.
Maybe it is important to believe in a place more empty
than the one we live in, though we often find, as some
astronomers have, some dark speck of sky suddenly exploding
with millions of stars from 170,000 years ago—
or in our desire to being again, we find a genetic Eve
below the Sahara who links us all by a shining necklace
of DNA, or the burning necklace of a tire in South Africa.
Maybe it is not chance but identity that frightens us.
Maybe, as you say, it is chance that saves us. Only a few miles
from John Griffin's lean-to is the painting by Dennis Carter,
"Covering the Retreat From Breed's Hill," which correctly
titles the misplaced battle of Bunker Hill and where every
face, British and American, is the same face. I don't know
if Carter was too poor to afford a model, or if perhaps
he painted himself everywhere on that terrible day,
realizing how in all wars it is ourselves we kill.

Did you know that the soldiers in the Old Granary Burial Ground
lie by a similar chance beneath the wrong headstones
realigned a hundred years ago without a plan?

In Golubac I thought the unmarked stones of the dead
meant, for once, that I did not have to remember the lost.
I watched the sheep being herded by a young boy.
I tried to repeat the Serbian names for fish.
I watched two lovers rise and pass over the hill.
Somewhere, later, it did not matter where, he would
bring her whatever part of the morning he owned,
spilling part of it from his hands the way, sometimes,
one of the other of us would. I have included him
because it seems only an accident he is not one
of the Partisans whom, I learned later, lost too many
to bury with a name, and not the son of one of the women
who were taken at random, six carloads of them,
from a town east of here, Mostar, taken by the Ustaca,
the arm of the Germans, taken for infidels and thrown
from cliffs hidden in the mountains, their bright skirts
making it appear as if some peasant had come to toss
the burning brush he cleared from his fields. Later,
one bishop praised the shining light of God at work.

Maybe everything is chance. I'm going to begin
all over again—I had started to tell you how the nail
I found, partially melted, was my father's souvenir from
Hiroshima where over forty years ago your mother
left a few days before the bomb's light while my father was
ordnance officer where the planes took off. I think
he meant the nail to say how easy it is to ignore or forget
the deaths. This morning I was looking at the pictures
survivors drew, childlike stick figures that try
to say what Carter's painting does about the self
we kill,—a horse standing blind and smoldering
among all those bodies, the children trying to nurse
from the dead mothers that shielded them still,
the hands of one boy hanging like rubber gloves,

another boy that looked like boiled octopus, the legs
of the women that looked like pomegranates. Even
those metaphors should tell us how we try to displace death
among our familiar objects—gloves, vegetables, fish—
to obscure from us whatever a life might mean.

Years ago, my father, who taught so much with a joke,
taught me the wrong way to set a boy's rabbit trap,
an old apple crate leaning against a stick, lettuce
or carrots underneath so that I couldn't pull the string
quickly enough, and the rabbit would disappear into the brush.
Instead, we built small houses for the birds, bee hives,
dog houses, shelters. Later, in the hills of Pownal, Vt.,
below where the moose Bullwinkle would appear, I met
Russ Vliet rebuilding an old farm, without electricity,
with a wood stove for heat, hammering straight,
as my father did, the bent nails that show how fragile
whatever holds the world together must be. Once, when
a white bee box spilled and the hive escaped, he said
it only followed the motions of the expanding universe
too fast for our sight to catch up—bits of ourselves
we lose each time we turn away. Now we hardly know
anymore what beginnings will hold our stories together, do we?

I am trying again. I have been watching a barn spider spin
an orb during the time I have written this, something it does
each day before withdrawing to a point above, waiting
for tremors, as if too much self would dissolve
the web. In sleep, my daughter in the next room
says a few casual words that could be a greeting
or farewell to someone who will never step out of her dream,
perhaps the young friend whose grave she's afraid to visit.
Today the news is all the young suicides for grief who mistake
one life for another, and I want to tell her not to be afraid.
And it is true, I have let you hide here in a pronoun,
and in places like Boston, Mostar, Vermont, Hiroshima,
maybe tomorrow in the words of one of your poets,
or the words of the scapular my daughter showed me. This is

no place for us to apologize for becoming the words we've spoken,
or for the disappearing story of our past. When they write
about landscapes, the hard, unfeeling hills that come
alive at dawn, Pavese and Vliet remind me how lucky
we are to be anyplace on earth. I am writing this
to anyone, to my father sitting alone, fingering
the bent nail he no longer remembers, to Russ, and to you
disappearing whenever I dream of you, wherever
you are,—I am going to trust you to go on living.
Just now, the light slakes off a swift's quick wings.
It is not the light of God, and not chance either.
I hope the peaceful ghosts of Golubac go on living as they have.
The fish, even now, are still pretending to be the dawn.
I hope their light is surfacing in you when this ghost arrives.

SELF PORTRAIT OF RIVARD BY JACKSON

I have an orchard full of tears.
I am passing through the eye of the needle.
I have abandoned my desire to be all the pronouns.
I have forgotten my loneliness in Arizona.
I am buying a house where the neighbors hang
their souls out on the line to dry.
Sometimes I feel like the Greek poet Philetas
who wore shoes of lead so he wouldn't fly away.
The dining room has three coats of paint.
I use a roller. My father uses a brush.
These are two basic ways you can see the cosmos.
Lucretius thought the sun was the size of a shield.
Anaxagoras was banished for impiety
when he suggested the sun was bigger
than Peloponnesus. If he were banished
to Arizona he would have watched
the long nosed bat, covered with white pollen,
seed the cactus flowers. I sat there
one night among the elf owls peering out
from their tiny nests. The desert is reincarnated
every night as your secret desire.
They have proven that the desert sparrow
navigates by reckoning gravity lines.
In 1555 the Bishop of Uppsala
declared that sparrows winter underwater.
Whole colonies of insects live their lives
on one branch of a tree in my backyard.
Even Plato came to love his cave.
My new house is only two blocks
from a decent jazz bar. I still have a little
work to do on the attic. I spent a long time
fixing the huge leak in the kitchen. Why is it
so difficult to use scissors with the left hand?
I have forgotten my loneliness in Arizona.
My poems were milling around the frontiers

waiting for visas. I was reading the billboards
of the heart. I was reading the stars.
Kepler thought the orbits of each planet
corresponded to Platonic forms. He wore
a baggy suit covered with soup stains
and made his living as a court astrologer.
His mother was carried away one night
in a laundry chest to be tried as a witch.
In one of his books he describes North Africa
as kissing the southern coast of Spain.
He was banished from Graz by some Bishop
but never lost his integrity. After he rushed
back to defend his mother she died of
a broken heart. My father is back in New Bedford.
Now I just retreat to my office.
How many bodies walk inside us as we walk?
My story has come a long way with holes
in its shoes. I don't know why I feel
compelled to reveal all this. I have a new house.
I have forgotten my loneliness in Arizona.

MY CRUELEST MUSE

If nothing else I still have this black Scripto
pencil, this notebook, and this hag of a muse
who hides out in the attic stirring an old hornets' nest,
who lets me live anyone's life but my own.
She was born years ago when my classmates were
mocking Ellen, nearly blind, pock-marked,
her spine twisted, but never gave me the strength
to fight for truth. She was there with her crowd
of laments, tearing their shirts, holding their arms
out to the sky. She was there when anyone
slipped under a car, forgot to wake up, caught
a bullet in some jungle. She was there carrying
flowers, telling me the way to cry. Jesus,
I loved that pain. I loved feeling bad
for the murderer everyone turned on at the movies.
I felt bad for the executioner whom I imagined
firing reluctantly. No one else knew his loneliness.
Imagine calling this love. Imagine you are
Caravaggio cursing the same muse we do.
In the shadows in the Church of St. Francis
in Rome I saw his *Calling of St. Matthew,*
saw Christ entering the dark tavern, extending
a hand to the foppish saint who is surrounded
by rogues who are plotting to cheat some soul.
Christ could be anyone, a highwayman demanding
money, and Matthew points to his own breast
as if to question or accuse himself. He must be
Caravaggio wondering why his own work is
ridiculed. Imagine the artist taking his models
not from some ideal, but from the victims
he robbed or cheated. I love to imagine him
lurking in the shadows he painted by night
in order to extend daylight across one face
or another that must have looked up in disgust
or horror. I love to see him walk in the blazing

streets first of Naples, then Malta, where he is
exiled for killing a noble in a duel. I love
the way he walks through the rain that is floating,
not falling, around him, the same rain he enters
on the road back to Rome, pardoned, the rain
that is filling the marshes to hide the malaria
that finishes him outside the walls. This was love,
this was living the life for art, cursing the muse.
If nothing else, this was blaming the nearest shadow
for our own cruelty, sitting around the tavern table
unable to act, wiping the blood off the soldier's
boots, oiling his guns, locking the cell doors
with each empty phrase, but this was also hoping
that even in the cruelest things we say there's
something we forget, a kind of miracle, a whisper
against the treacherous night, the way Matthew's
companion, slumped over his beer in the corner, is
ready to lift his head, ready maybe to write the poem
he always avoided, ready to take the blame.

EIGHT BALL

Every time I tried to put the eight ball
in a corner pocket, memory knocking feebly
at the door on such a night, every time I scratched,
I looked up to see the same drops of rain
repeating themselves outside, while inside, the air
full of the gypsy smoke Lorca would have sung to,
they were never going to stop dancing, not going
to stop feeding quarters to the jukebox
to hear Willie Nelson and Ray Charles do
Seven Spanish Angels. These were Lorca's old peasants
in those poems about desperate love,
death in red suspenders and new jeans,
hope, maybe older, in a big frill blouse,
doing the two-step for half the night, celebrating love
while time lingered over a mint julep at the bar.

In 1963 Brother Linus was teaching us the principles
of a chain reaction with billiard balls. Back then
the days were counterfeit and easy to spend.
Time was a forest of dried flowers. In 1986
it was Lorca's morning glory the woman had pinned
in her hair, a little flowering weed snatched from love's
buttonhole, and their table was filled with yellow jessamine,
white aster, bluebells, passion flowers
they must have picked themselves, all those poems
with flowers, the poems *were* flowers,
Lorca wrote once, *a garden of possibilities,*
and the words were butterflies always moving away,
walking to the park at 5:00 p.m. because, he wrote once,
that was *the hour the gardens begin to suffer.*

This late, boredom was racking up the balls.
This late it was Willie Mosconi waltzing around the table
towards another run, surrounded by headless shadows,
it was The Hustler, it was Minnesota Fats and Fast

Eddy Felsen racking them up all night, the world on hold,
taking the blue chalk in one hand, twisting fate
over the tip of the stick, setting down the chalk in
one sure motion on the table without taking your eyes
from the perfect shot taking shape on the table below you.
It was desperation in its ragged coat.
It was the decaying radium glow of the ceiling lights.
It was luck stamping its feet, the dog at the bar
not bothering to raise its head, cursing each missed shot
of our own lives, cursing the Falangists
who gunned down Lorca and buried him in a nameless field.

But that night it was chance calculating the physics for
a perfect combination shot to the side pocket.
It has been thirty years since it was first proposed
that electrons follow every possible path
through the layers of parallel universes we live in at one time.
It is true that each universe is a kind of pool pocket
we are trying to enter with one of desire's elaborate shots.
It is true that electrons tunnel from one pocket to another.
Which brings me to 1965, New York
on the steps of the same building Lorca lived in,
singing Spanish songs so badly it budged
the old men in their only clothes from the Harlem steps.
The only girl I remember kept my vase of purple flowers,
railroad vines whose tracks led beyond
the Long Island beaches where I found them
in some lovers' graveyard, the small hollow
in the dunes scattered with sticky
tissues, cigarette butts, used condoms, underwear,
and those petals strewn about that must have flowered
in someone's hair. I waited for hours trying
to glimpse into another universe. I just sat there
behind the brush while the steamers were
heading towards places with names that never seemed real.

Now we were covered with blue chalk dust looking like
big flowers, larkspurs, maybe, absurd irises,

and the old couple who never heard of Garcia Lorca were
listening to the plaintive songs of Patsy Cline, they were
weathering whatever loneliness they feared,
they were going to dance again, to keep quarters
in the jukebox, calling yesterday back
just as she was almost out the door,
calling her back with all her friends
and their empty bottles of whatever, their jessamine,
the bluebells on the table in front of them.

I was going to play it safe on a night when nothing
had been falling for me, on a night when I took up
the stick again for a last rack, when the little second hand
on the clock hesitated between leaps. I was going to
nudge the cue ball to the far cushion then let it glance
back to the triangle of balls for this break—let someone
else make the mistakes this time, but I looked up instead
from a perfect cross corner shot, the only one
I'd make all night, and you were gone, you were disappearing
with that one lost moment of perfect grace into the rain,
and I was still facing the scattered table that didn't seem real
any longer, thinking *this is how it ends*, both of us
lost by then, but I was brushing the blue chalk off
for good, I was trying to figure which way you had gone,
trying to recall the name of that purple flower,
one universe filling the pockets of the next, Lorca gone,
time slipping off the barstool, leaving it swiveling,
the words of Lorca's general echoing through the rain,
coffee, give him plenty of coffee, by which he meant death,
the holy electrons, the lost worlds, all of them going on.

III

A Robin Red breast in a Cage
Puts all Heaven in a Rage.
A dove house fill'd with doves & Pigeons
Shudders Hell thro' all its regions.
A dog starved at the Masters Gate
Predicts the ruin of the State.

—Blake

A LETTER FROM THE OUTDOOR CAFE
AT THE LIPIZZANER STUD FARM,
VILENICA, SLOVENIA

A number of cultures have possessed memory bags which consisted of articles with smells that brought back memories from the past, smell being the most nostalgic of our senses.

Here are those stories still straggling back with the partisans,
abandoning their equipment by the side of the road.
Through the smoke of days the yellow orchids from the swamps
around Ljubljana were bent over the way your Ana would,
working the fields. It was an age when someone else's eyeglasses
encircled the world. She was trying to harvest a little tenderness
under a moon that had suspected everything all along.
You could still hear the Nazis
stealing whatever flowers they wanted from the market
near the Dragon bridge to toss
on the naked body of some girl they would finish with.
All the streets had been barricaded with fear.
The sun went walking on the water, saving no one.
When we met, the past had been playing its terrible game of leapfrog.
The night was putting on its gloves.
There was the stench of betrayal, the shy story
straining at the buttonholes of the heart.
There was the must of the spider whose web
caught our stories between the trellis and the drainpipe
whenever the waiter approached, whenever suspicion
would grab the grating from where it hid in the sewer.
There were the white clouds of Lipizzaners clattering their way
over the asphalt road to the stables. There was a tiny green lizard,
all that was left of a lover's hand gliding up your arm.
There was this: the story we invented of the girl unable to leave
because she had left something behind in her lover's dream—
map, shoe, comb, distance, reasons. There is probably
a little snow from the streetlamp holding
the few flakes like a child's glass toy. A few days later
her hands reach from the slats of a box car.
She had been busy trying to tame the stars.

Meanwhile the heavy odor of horses cantered from the stable.
Every once in a while the waiter's red vest signalling the spider
of silence. Faith forging its names on the checks we would pay with.
How he must have touched her that last night,
the overwhelming odor of her sex, her body so luminous
he thought his hand must have passed right through her,
must have touched her so long, delaying, that they believed
they inhabited someone's left over dream.
She was so wet he must have lived inside her most of that night.
Later, some trouble in the stables, a worker knocked down
by a stallion or the terrano he was drinking. The waiter's
red vest went lurking around the dumpster.
He was not so unlike your jailer in that age when your words
had to be stacked with the firewood behind the shed.
Here was a threshold without a door the day could leave by.
We were praising William Harvey, 1578–1657,
for describing the simple circulation of the blood.
Later our wine was discussing the despair of the last Mayans,
Hannibal's dreams, the discovery of those new moons around Neptune,
our spider's knowledge of nuclear geometry, the proper way
to add sea grass to slivovitz, of Stalin's fears, the secret desires
of Achilles. Drago said the Lipizzaner horses are
descendents of the famous ones Achilles mocked
for their failure to imagine another end for him.
He said to write this. It is all imagination and possibility. It is all memory.
He said the story we invented was yours. It is filled with the odor
of terrano. It stands for restless years in the stable of dreams.
What does it mean for the night when the crow slumps his head to
        one wing?
When will the lover's ear be filled with honeysuckle?
What does it mean when the wind refuses to caress your arm?
When the water refuses to level itself as Newton predicted?
What does it mean to inhabit this left-over dream?
The lizards were the reflected futures scurrying around the cafe.
But the lover, the lover took the train back to the village
where he found the verbs had blackened everything into the past.
The dead were frozen into all the fantastic positions for lovemaking.
It was so cold there was no odor to remember. He could imagine

each life frozen for a moment in the acrid oil of the gun barrel.
In the distance, joy stumbling through a field of foxholes.
In the distance, the white clouds would be white clouds again.
The red vest dangling its keys at that late hour.
Achilles, it is said, died friendless on the plains of Troy.
For days he could smell the funeral fire of Patroclus.
In the distance the long caravan of memories, the candle blacks
the lovers take in after one has turned to pinch the flame,
the smell of the first squint of light, and the last,
the odor of grief, and despair, these odors that stay with us longer
even than our memories for them, these odors I am sending you now
because I have heard the news from Drago—they have taken your son—
because the horses are flying again, leaving behind their rich nitrogen,
because maybe the orchids are lifting their faces, maybe the moon
no longer suspects us, because any love is terrifying by its loss,
but so also is the loss of memory, the pure loneliness of the imagination.

THE SUM OF THE DRAFTS EXCEEDS THE WHOLE

It wasn't long ago that this poem began with a cough,
with a sneeze, with a little too much pollen in the air,
it began with the pollen my father said started the watery
eyes, the blindness that was the real reason he shot
the rudder off his own dive bomber at gunnery school,
Orlando, Florida, 1943, and the real reason he got
the desk job for the rest of the war keeping track of
the planes they were afraid he might shoot down. It wasn't
long after that opening that the poem began with the image
of wind rustling through the ponderosa pines near the Yuba river
where I panned for gold a hundred and fifty years too late,
the sound of the pines and the sound of the water being
the same sound, and later, 35,000 feet above those pines
in an airplane I knew my father couldn't shoot down,
I realized these lines don't belong in this poem
anyways. But in a universe that will eventually contract,
sending time backwards, we will all be collecting
our previous mistakes. "It goes without saying,"
another draft began, and it did. And here are
those lines left in an umbrella rack a few nights ago.
And here, a few impoverished images whose eyes
open like wallets. Now the drafts become a little
indecisive. The poem is about to present a choice
as in one of those "Write Your Own Adventure" books:
"If you take the first tunnel on the left, go to
line 37," "If you climbed into the fighter plane,
the poem may never end." Behind each word another
word will lurk, behind each sentence, too many choices.
So where does it go? maybe it returns to the image
of water—"The world is water," someone says jokingly,
but the poem knows this is true, knows all about Thales
the Greek philosopher who described the origins of all
matter as water—the watery table, watery sky,
watery rock—even my father's watery eyes and the fifty
caliber machine gun. There is a growing confidence

that the water image can stand for anything later on.
So the poem tries to tell you again about its own past,
and who wouldn't, given the right time and our loneliness.
But it realizes something you don't: "you" has
nothing to refer to if you are not reading
this line. And that's the trouble, really, there is
so little we can hold that we want to refer to later on.
Decades ago the astronomer Harlow Shapely erased
what he thought were mistakes from a photographic
plate of Andromeda that tell us today why the universe is
still expanding. He couldn't imagine galaxies
beyond our own. Even this poem in its oddball way is
trying to compensate for losses it knows too well.
Earlier, like you, it climbed into that fighter plane,
glided through the clear water of the sky, the currents
of the Yuba river, flew through the rain to Santiago,
Chile, where the women danced with pictures of the dead
and missing the government refused to refer to,
where the real planes of the real air force threatened.
Hardly any idea has escaped its concern in some
earlier draft; it remembers how in Salvador
two gunmen from the death squads, with silencers,
gunned down the pacifist Herbert Anaya in front of
his children. The poem is unable to offer excuses
for this sudden change of tone—one image simply
follows another in a flight as unpredictable as the paper
planes my father would make, tilting a wing here
trying to remember a funny story about gunnery school, tilting
there to find a story about dying, and you have probably
anticipated how this could go anywhere next—to 1971,
to the fish trying to become a crescent moon at the end
of my father's line, too small to keep, and the sadness,
my father's incredible sadness that its leap would fail
the way the sparks between his own neurons had begun
to fail also that summer, the summer I was drafted,
the summer he said *don't go, don't leave,* waiting
for the stars to drain out of Corbett's pond that dawn.
Today I am standing above the trees, floating

one paper airplane out after another from the porch,
watching them glide perfectly through the branches,
towards anyone the poem thought of and discarded,
to wherever the watery currents will take them,
to wherever my father must have headed
his last few days, flying solitary in bed,
his compass broken, the maps gone,
the old stories flaming out over some nameless atoll,
because I am realizing in these last few lines
that this is another elegy, after all, leaving
only itself, leaving words behind words, offering
no excuses, take it, tilting a wing that signals
what love is, what I forgot to say, as simple
as a flock of stars, how they break formation,
how they form again when all the light seemed lost.

SHADOWS

Why is there something rather than nothing?
—Parmenides

What a consoling poem this will be if the roadside
crows that scatter into pines as each car passes,
that rise like the souls of the dead in Van Gogh's wide
and confused heaven, are not the signs of your loss.
What a consoling poem this might be if I could remember
the first secret place where the pitiful world did not,
as Flaubert says it does, surface in terrible error
like the bloated bodies of dogs in a stream near his retreat
at Rouen, those poor shadows of the dead, despite
the stones tied to their necks, and surface in the sentences
Flaubert wrote trying to find a secret place for each right
word, a place that did not mean the old disgust for happiness.
I thought I had seen death. I see instead those rising crows
again, remember your leaving, and, scattered here, in shadows
that fall across this page, figures I'd forgotten, shadows
that seem to rise from the faded newsprint, that seem to show
how each private loss is part of a larger loss we might
remember,—yesterday's news is the young boy in Providence
R.I., who followed the consoling words of some killer one night
into woods where animals later tore off his face, or two Palestinians,
two boys, faces covered, who followed one street or another
with a crowd of protesters and were shot, or how, unable to let
death take him, a Bantu tribesman clutched the dirt of his father,
lifting himself again so the Pretoria soldiers could not forget.
Listen, it is nearly dawn here. I wish all these losses
could hide in the shifting forms of these words, that you could hide
in their dream that tries to tell you not to abandon your past
in a few clothes on the shore, no place left to hide.

I didn't know, when you left, about poor Flaubert never finding
the words to dominate the absurd sounds of parrots he kept
hearing, the plaintive sounds of cicadas that always haunted
him, how he would mutilate phrases, how he'd shift sentences,
how each word was, he wrote, an "endless farewell to life,"

crossing out repetitions that meant he had only one voice,
that meant, really, hearing the endless terror of his own voice.
I didn't know, then, about Van Gogh, who was finding
in an asylum, while Flaubert tried to write an asylum for his life,
a style to hold off death, a style that he feared, that he kept
even from his brother. I hadn't read, then, those poor sentences
to Theo, haunted by the power of color and shape, haunted
by shadows of enemies he invented, the way the birds haunt
his last painting, *Crows Over a Wheatfield*, where the lost voice
of Christ seems to dissolve into darkness that moment his sentence
was finished, those crows that could be flying towards us, finding
only our losses, or up towards heaven, or maybe they keep
wavering, flying both ways at once, the way Van Gogh's life
would, as he himself knew, painting, he wrote, his own life
in theirs. I can't help but wonder how those crows haunt
all his last paintings. I believe he must have found a way to keep
a secret place somewhere on each canvas, the way Christ's voice
seems to hide beneath the thick paint. I believe he must have found
how the birds carry the painting away from itself, as Flaubert's sentences
were meant to lead him away from what he called the sentence
of his life. And because he saw a halo shimmering around each life
or object the way he had as a young preacher, what did Van Gogh find,
what consolation against all that pain? I am still haunted
by that faceless boy in Providence, the African without a voice,
the Palestinian boys kept from their homes, these deaths that keep
announcing their obscene selves. Like Flaubert, I'm going to keep
trying to find some style, some shape for these sentences.
I believe I can hear, in Van Gogh's painting, the poor voice
of Christ which is the voice, too, of Flaubert, and these lost lives
that haunt me now. I believe that the last demon that haunted
Van Gogh was his fear that, outside his frames, nothing was found
to keep the "troubled skies" from his life, nothing even
in his sentences to Theo—"what's the use?" he asked hauntingly,
finally, like the voice of Christ, crying to be found.

Listen, I am writing to you now, on this table crossed
by shadows, that the answer is anyone hearing your voice,
anyone hoping the next news of you is not your loss,

trying by these repetitions to call you back, though the place
keeps shifting because I can't hide the world Flaubert, at Rouen,
fought inside each phrase, and you wouldn't believe a story
with no form for suicide or death. Here I am again
thinking of Van Gogh, listening to Lightnin' Hopkins say
the blues are everywhere, the blues are us, these stories
he sings on the scratched tape, the stories we read
about Van Gogh, the headlines, the poems, the way
the blues rhythms never change, 4/4, as if we needed
something that constant against our fears, as if we knew
how much these sad stories showed us what it means
to go on. Here I am again, listening to the blues,
starting to understand it is my own despair I mean
to fight. Last night, I stood on the bridge where a friend
dove into the shadows of the Tennessee and was afraid
I understood. I was thinking of the faceless boy again,
remembering how the man who found him by the pond where he lay
face down, turned him over, saw what the animals had done
and knelt in prayer, knelt for the pity of it, for the faces
of everyone dead or missing, knowing how he must go on.
I was thinking, too, how the mothers of the Palestinian boys
must also have knelt, must have touched the life
leaking from them, must also have prayed, unwrapped
the cloth around their heads hoping some other life,
not a son's, was missing. I have been thinking how the map
of this table, ever since you left, scatters the shadows
of fears this poem tries to shape, and how Van Gogh's
pictures, the dark secret places in Flaubert's phrases, show
all our words as a care for life, a color we have to hold.

I can't forget that faceless boy. I can't stop wondering
what last thing he touched or saw. I get up, punch
another tape into the player, Charlie Parker, "the Bird,"
taking off into rhythms and harmonies more unpredictable
than Van Gogh's crows—taking notes from what he touched or saw—
dogs barking, the hiss of a radiator, the sudden squeal
of a train's brakes, the rhythm and harmonies of the unpredictable
drunk shifting in a doorway, changing every sad thing

so that the dog's barking, the hiss of the radiator, the squeal
of brakes becomes not a sign of loneliness or loss, but joy,
the notes shifting like Flaubert's words, like the drunk in the doorway,
discovering in each phrase and note some secret place
among the flattened fifths meaning either loss or joy,
among the odd intervals of chords his alto sax remembers,
until he fell asleep for good in an armchair in New York,
nearly 35, "I'm just a husk," he said, in the end, just a phrase
or interval you remember, and I do, in this poem for you,
taking these hints from the flights of the bird, Charlie Parker,
who lived beyond death in each note, each husk, each phrase,
above the deaths of the boy, the Palestinians, the tribesmen.

I remember last summer, finding an old sax player
just waking among the remnants of fieldstone cellars
some quarry workers left half a century ago outside
Gloucester, Mass., a place called *Dogtown*, where he tried
among the sounds of stray dogs Parker would have loved
to remember the clear notes of the alto sax rising above
the trees, above his memory of the war, unable to sleep
without checking the perimeter, each hour, to keep
all the shadows named and held, unable to sleep at all
if it rained because he couldn't hear the enemy's footfall.
It could have been you there, he said, and I know,
I know all our shadows, *it could have been you.*
And I am remembering the Bantu tribesman, how he could
tell immediately that the difference between dirt and blood
no longer mattered, that the lost children he fought for,
the child detained for questioning and found weeks later
among the smoldering garbage, his tongue cut out
for talking to newsmen, were what his death might be about,
a death that gathered above the tin roofs as the past gathered
—maybe the way it gathered in the eyes of the sax player
who could not forget, as he told it, the way his base
camp was overrun, the way, after a while, the haze
he was seeing was not dawn, not even the smoke of rifles,
but the unbelievable smoke of bodies burning, and the terrible
vapor that rose from open wounds, the sickening stink

that took the place of words, screams, whatever he tried to think.
When things were bad, he said, he could remember the service
for William Williams in New Orleans, how the entire brass
had gathered for the long march to Carrolton cemetery—
the Eureka Brass Band—with it slow dirges, its heavy
hymn notes to "In the Sweet Bye and Bye," the trombones
leading the way, he and his father among the baritone
horns of the second rank—and how they danced on the way
home to "St. Louis Blues," music, he said, you could raise
the dead with, as now, he just wanted once more to hear
the consoling notes of Parker, some sound to drive away his fear.

Listen, I have tried to find for us a shape for all this grief,
a form to make, as Parker and Van Gogh did, our fear
into a strength. It may be that any form is a kind of belief
that the losses, the shadows on this table, the enemy we fear
when the world goes dark, can be contained beyond our moment.
In Berea, Ohio, once, I came across an old graveyard
next to a quarry, centered by a concubine pine, a tree
that grew around its own cones and branches that were bent
around the trunk, as if the tree took as its form the discarded
parts of its own past and future. Now I want to believe
the long embrace of that tree, to touch my hands to your face,
I am touching my own face now, unable to forget that faceless
boy, the frightened sax player, hoping to find here some place
where we can kneel before these shadows, where we can bless
and embrace our pasts. I am blessing the past of a friend, torn coat,
hovering on a doorstep in Belgrade before he escaped the Russians,
who would twist gunpowder out of shells to sell to gangs for bread,
who watched a kneeling soldier smile to slit a prisoner's throat,
who chose not the Danube, but life. Not long ago I knelt in
the park where he played, one secret place where finally the dead
were only distant shadows. I was feeding the few ragged crows
that could have been Van Gogh's birds, leaving them a little bread
and cheese, thinking again of you, of your sadness, of how
form may be only, as Whitman said, another name for the body,
for all the secret places we contain, the only consolation we
    have known—

and I was gathering you around me, building my own secret place inside you, feeling you move again unpredictably, like Parker's rhythms, the shifts in Flaubert's sentences, knowing, having known, that this poem begins in your body and ends in the same place, feeling the world move, trying to stay this way forever.

VICTOR HUGO'S *HUNCHBACK OF NOTRE DAME* BY RICHARD JACKSON

There's a door that begins with a hole in the heart.
There are these old feelings I carry on a chain.
There are little cloisters of darkness in the light.
There is the desire of the rain for the willow's roots.
There is a cathedral—I was elected *The Pope of Fools.*
Its gutters are too small to capture the overflow of history.
Light lances the windows like a Roman soldier.
There must be sounds, but they have folded
themselves into petals for the night.
There's someone who will leave the door open
so Death walks in chomping his cigar like a union boss.
There is Esmeralda who gives the moon its light.
For now Death just opens the refrigerator door
letting the light spill out as if it were milk,
reading the old novels he's insanely devoted to.
There's a storm breaking out deep in his mind.
There's the archdeacon falling from the drainpipe.
There's Victor Hugo who spent 20 years in exile.
You can see Rodin's statue in a park in Paris.
He tied the rope around the gypsy's neck.
She wasn't a gypsy. She was an angel.
When she danced he thought she was a witch
for what she made him think. Why is the world
always passing beyond the rim of our eyes?
Why would anyone think she was a witch?
There's a woman in New Mexico who saw
the image of Jesus on a tortilla she burned
in a skillet in 1977. There's Arlene Gardner
who saw him on her freezer in East Springs,
Tennessee, ten years later. Now they are saints.
Why is the sun always asleep in your heart?
There's this face, this body, no one can argue.
But there's Tycho Brahe who wore a metal nose
from a duel. All he could do was measure.

He understood nothing. He shook the stars
like dice to guide him. Now he's a saint.
He died from an infected bladder
because he was too polite to leave the table.
There's the way my gypsy hung against
that roulette wheel of the moon. There are
the years I lay beside her sifting into dust.
There's a casual breeze rolling a few cigarettes in the alley.
And there's Death, it's your door he's entering now.
He's playing jacks for the random moments
you have already forgotten. You thought
you could take off the past like a pair of socks.
There's the blood in his veins which is smoke.
There are blackbirds disguising themselves as stars.
There's the way he throws finger shadows
on the old calender tacked to the wall
trying to imitate the shapes he's taken
against the cathedral door. My own spine
happens to aim at the sky like a dogwood.
There are the hoofs of someone else's story
always clattering through the city gates.
There's the rain bringing its memories
of what happens higher up.
The dust is already settling in my dreams.
There's a suitcase beside a road afraid to go on.
I'm not saying it's mine. I'm not saying it's yours.
There's all those dying planets gnawing on their bones.
There's a little stain of blood on the floor of heaven.

TRUE OR FALSE

I have abandoned my life as a trapeze artist.
I will no longer hang my net from star to star.
Sept. 6, 1991, and I am push-starting Boris' Renault 4
down a hill into another era, swinging from the open
door to the roof bar as if I were one of the flying
Romanovs. It is 500 million years after
the increase in our oxygen led to skeletal animals.
A few hills behind us the Serbs are lobbing bombs
at a few Croatian churches. We are tracking a fugitive
future the way those aborigines in Australia follow
the dream paths that scientists think are the lines
of magnetic fields. They pause on a ridge, the last
drops of light soaking into the ground, listening
for the footsteps of old words kicking up a few stones
in front of them. Now the night begins its gossip
about the day. The important thing is to let
the momentum of your swing carry you smoothly,
without straining to reach, or you will break
the aerodynamic flow and miss the bar altogether.
Do you think we will make it all the way to Lipica?
Each time I enter a new dream of you, I find someone
has tampered with it. The world is only as true
as what you see through a commander's binoculars.
Therefore, I have abandoned my desire to fit
all my angels on the head of a pin. Over 96%
of visible matter is hydrogen or helium. Tank traps
litter the side of our road like a huge game of jacks some giant
has abandoned. The body of the giant, Cormoran,
lies at Dinusul, England, which just happens to sit
on a bardic dream path as ancient as those of the aborigines,
and includes Stonehenge and Glastonbury Abbey
where in 1539 Henry VIII hung, drew and quartered
the last abbot, Richard Whiting, while preparing to marry
his fourth wife. In that year Spain annexed Cuba.
Also, the first Christmas tree was introduced at Strasburg.

Why have I always been fascinated with dates?
This little Renault 4 can do over 80 in fourth gear.
Maybe I should abandon my desire to peek through
the keyholes of history. I have already abandoned
my desire to do a triple twist somersault
back through my own formative years. Maybe
I should just lie quietly inside you while our old selves
slip in and out of the back rooms of the soul.
Or maybe Descartes was right—we each become
two people, avoiding clandestine meetings
with ourselves. There are some people who try to arrange
their lives so they don't even have to be present.
Maybe that's why Rumor has wandered out of Vergil,
out of the fires and rubble of Carthage, only to huddle
under a streetlight in its oversized coat, studying the maps,
trying to find its way past the shanties of our hearts,
trying to find a life in the files of some general.
In a few minutes, we will pass this wreck and traffic
will flow smoother. Why do they always pull a coat
over the face of the old man who has been struck?
In Brazil, the boy who was born without a face
gradually had the few parts that were there arranged,
the rest being invented by the doctors until by now
everything has been done but incomplete. Only
the shallow, as Oscar Wilde said, will ever know themselves.
Maybe I should abandon everything except a few harmless
details. We can just rest awhile in one of these
loopholes of the wind. I can stroke the soft petal of your belly.
No car. No war. No lies. The kind of life enjoyed
by broccoli in cheese sauce. Did you know that
horseback riding began in the Ukraine 6,000 years ago?
That there are 2 million atoms of nickel for every
four of silver in our galaxy? That Bernie Doyle and I
cut half a day in the 3rd grade coat room before
the nuns found us? If I pile up enough of these facts
we can all just forget about the truth. I remember
swinging from prank to prank along the ladder
on our schoolyard jungle gym. The curious thing

about the Renault 4 is that the gear shift is built
into the dashboard. Only 17% of Americans believe
Elvis is still alive. Believe me when I say that trapeze
artists are very big in this part of the world. In 1950
Edgar Rice Burroughs died while reading the comic pages.
That was about the time a whole flock of regrets started
descending over Croatia. In the third century the emperor
of China was buried with 6,000 individualized clay soldiers.
In 1980 Libya ordered England off its maps creating
a new arm of the North Sea. It would have taken more
than my incredible repertoire of aerial acrobatics
to avoid the train loads of errors shipped to us over time.
Like the TV detective of my childhood I just want the facts.
In 1955 the nuns marched us across the street from
St. Patrick's school to attend the wake of a classmate.
I had not yet abandoned my love for Maureen Brennan.
I bought my first telescope and saw my first binary star.
I leaned over, as I was told, to kiss the side of his face
not covered by bandages to hide the cancer.
On Mount St. Helens, patches of flowers are growing
out of ash in the shape of decayed animals that died there.
If we ever wrecked this tin car we'd be dead.
For thirty years I couldn't attend another funeral.
On Sept 6, 1991 in Croatia seven men are laid out
by the side of the road like burnt wicks, throats cut,
testicles jammed into their mouths. For 30 years
I believed my friend, Bernie Doyle, had moved away,
but it was him, wasn't it, in that casket in 1955.
Every day, it seems, another dream is chained
to the cell wall. Even the flowers have put on
their gray trenchcoats. 12 billion light years from here
a gas cloud 100 times the size of the Milky Way is
getting ready to form a second generation of stars
from the elements of millions of supernovas,
which means that all life begins in a kind of fog
and no matter how many times we start over
we will never see clearly enough. Therefore,
I am abandoning my life as a fish, my reptilian brain,

even my allegiance to the lower animals. What we are is
62,000 miles of capillaries if we care to line them up.
It seems like every galaxy is tumbling through space
as if it, too, had missed in its grab for the bar.
According to the laws of entropy the more I write
the less true it all becomes. In fact, only the autobiographical
parts of this poem are true. Maybe we are just the abandoned
drafts of something better. Why had it taken me thirty years
to abandon my dream for Bernie? When we get to Lipica
I am going to clean the windshield. I will abandon
my communications with life on other planets. I abandon
the net, the chalk of a sure grip on these details,
the wristband that braced me against desire. Maybe our dearest
truths are shoes we abandon in some old dumpster. In 1910
thousands of people bought gas masks to protect
themselves from the cyanide in the tail of Halley's Comet.
In 1578 the Bishop of Magdeburg revealed that a comet is
the thick smoke of our sins. If this were true
the night sky ought to be a good deal brighter. If this car
doesn't make it all the way to Lipica we will have
to abandon it next to one of those burnt-out trucks
that stopped the tanks. I can still see the red freckles
covering Bernie's face. We had to write something
forgettable 1,000 times for skipping class. We will have
to wait for the night to slip back into its burrows.
Maybe we should forget about Lipica and head for Piran
and its topless beach. It is the home of the composer
Giovanni Tartini (1692-1770) who wrote *The Devil's Trill
Sonata* which might as well be our theme song. Besides,
it seems our Renault 4 has taken a wrong turn somewhere
and we must abandon everything. Boris himself will invent us
from the smell of abandoned fruit stands. We will spend
the rest of the day inventing a kind of love that no longer
exists in the world, a kind of love no army can pillage
at the outposts, no rumor could bring to its knees like a traitor,
no heart will leave abandoned at the crossroads. Here
Truth is lounging beneath a great oak, waiting to bum

another ride. Somewhere, a nameless
star is collapsing, but its light won't stop arriving,
it won't ever stop arriving for millions of years.

HISTORY

As if all history could fit inside a word.
In the car up on blocks in my neighbor's yard.
In the shopping cart the woman is living out of
from the park to the railroad bridge, alongside
the pigeons, the milk trucks, the sooty dawn,
always on the move. There's a dog, too, chained up,
so we can cross here beneath a sky already in pieces.
Today the Pioneer space probe is how many million
miles farther than the last time we checked.
A guerilla attack on some isolated village
somewhere in Angola for a few head of cattle.
It is only dawn but it already looks like rain.
Someone's in the car, I can hear them giggling,
my young self in what looks like the old
1955 Buick Special my father bought used,
a real bomb, but I can't recognize the girl
whose face is hidden from the future, her voice
is older than anything it says—rock, star,
tree, river, hill, turning into the names of gods.
It is 1958 and they are testing bombs in the Utah
desert, the dust drifting eastward, towards us.
What we want is rain to wash it all away.
What we want is one of those rivers Ovid lets
some goddess become conveniently. Beside it,
we will find Blake's lions and lambs
etched against a backdrop of trees. They are
covered by wild tendrils of words. They are
the first to feel the shock waves in the earth.
Actually astronomers tell us the whole
planet is wobbling badly if we could only
sense it. We'd better be careful not to knock
over the cinder blocks. We'd better put on
the heart's eyeglasses. Blake and his wife
would sit nude in their garden to shock
their friends. The dog is loose, and so now

we'll have to tell the truth to get out of here.
One negotiator puts a thumb into a cup
of soup to taste it, says the bombers will fly
if there's a break in the weather. In the end,
they follow Icarus out of myth into history.
All day we keep sending out signals like little
Pioneers. We keep trying to bump into some
planet or person and raise a little dust cloud,
leave some plaque or flag. Today is only
a passing thought I had back then, peeking
over the car window, throwing rocks at us kids
trying to move in for a closer look. Sometimes
it is possible to glimpse history as she licks
the tip of a finger to turn a page, a moment
when the car seems like the whole world except
that it is skidding sideways, as out of control
as ever, towards a group in front of the market
who suddenly understand how a whole course
of events depends upon such details.
One of them glances at the bruised sky.
Rain all morning. Rain all afternoon.

ACKNOWLEDGMENTS

I would like to begin by thanking the chaotic
shifting of neurons which is what allows our brains
to respond to stimuli flexibly and so to create
an order for what we never understand.
I would like to acknowledge that time
when the whole world was asleep in our throats.
I don't want to say too much about about those old days
that are always just chumming around the barrels
warming their hands, reciting the old complaints.
But I would like to acknowledge Kevin's story which
you could search for inside each of the following lines
the way a subatomic physicist
searches for a particle someone has named "top,"
the twin of "bottom," which is the hypothesis
that will explain the origins of the world.
What if there were no hypothetical questions?
They are the conditional tenses we use
to excuse the wrong choices we made.
For instance, this sentence would be nine words long
if it were six words shorter. Or this, from Mark Twain:
Wagner's music is better than it sounds. Dear reader,
I digress, I, too, can hear patience
dusting his spurs in the doorway.
Even now the hour begins to lean on its broken crutch.
So it is about time I acknowledged
the stone's desire to walk,
the wind's desire to gain visibility the way it did
in those smoky days when the first chemicals were
beginning to learn how to breathe.
I would like to include everything that has brought me
to this pitiful moment. In fact, if I had said all this earlier
everything we are now experiencing
would have taken place four minutes ago.
So I would like to acknowledge a scene
that is meaningful only to me

where my eight-year-old body is sprawled out
beside Kevin's on the rug beneath my aunt's Philco TV,
with its beveled mahogany, its electric smell of tubes
warming up. I can smell her wooden matches curl
around themselves inside her sea shell ashtrays.
I would like to thank Range Rider but it was
not him, really, and not Sky King, not Mister Wizard
but our own dreams we dragged through the dust of the news.
I might as well mention the woman preacher
on the radio from Memphis offering tapes
from the dead, $15.95, postage included.
Dear reader, please forgive these minor digressions
the way you forgive the dumb gaze of fish,
but I only want to remind myself how premature death is,
the way history gets folded and blurred in your pocket only
to be remembered later when you find some loose change.
How could we know the trees were shedding their leaves
inside us? That's why someone always leaves the light on
trying to hold everything in the room as it was.
So, I would like to acknowledge each hypothetical
version of this story where, say, the sky flees to another scene,
where shadows hardly ever fit their objects, where Kevin
and I would watch Kirk Douglas play Odysseus tearing
through the embers of Troy, where a moon's skull burned
in the sky, where we cut shields from plywood, nailed
handguards to our broomstick swords, where we never
listened to the lost songs of birds, nor, further than we
imagined, to the heels of the hanged beginning to clap
in our dreams, where an ambush of stars hid behind each tree.
At every turn we threatened the wind and the moon.
At every turn the branches were grabbing for the sky.
At every turn the landscape took the shape of whatever
dream would lap the dawn. We were looking for a city to burn.
I would like to acknowledge Tex Ritter for each Saturday matinee
where I helped clear the dozen black hats from the widow's ranch,
saving her future. I wish I could report that I saved Kevin's too.
Does it mean anything that the facts are never enough,
not even these diversions? The best description of bread is

one of hunger, the best description of a life is someone else's.
So then, I should like to mention Goya's "Searching for the Teeth,"
how the desperate Gypsy, out of modesty and shame,
holds a cloth over the left side of her face, turns away
as she pulls the gold from the mouth of the hanged man,
because for a moment, I am her, trying to imagine the story
she will tell: how the metal becomes part of the foil
to an archbishop's altar, candles blazing, or the lip of
the king's cup, the same king who forces Goya into exile
where he will die in Bordeaux. I would like to acknowledge
this story even if it is a lie, as long as it lets her live on.
Even back then Kevin and I knew that if the night was cold
it was because the stars wouldn't listen to each other.
We were looking for a song to sling over our shoulders.
We were looking for a coin to press into the palm of the moon.
And the Gypsy? Later we find her
clutching the wrapped fish she's stolen from a fishmonger
who has been paying off the police, shoving fruit into
her pockets. There is a light rain darkening the brows,
and we could meet her on that street, be surprised
at her beauty, and even, if we think long enough,
her innocence. You can gauge how important all this is
by how much my words have had to lie, to joke,
to hang around under streetlights smoking,
pretending to be the ghost of Munch
hanging his pictures in the Black Forest to rot,
reading the tabloids, faking the science,
using words like pi meson, neutrino, graviton
to hide behind because, in the end, each of these words
or ideas is only a fiction, a sign for a version
I shouldn't ever reveal. But first, I would like to thank
the park attendant with his spiked cane trying
to pick up the footprints Kevin and I left that summer,
and for the way he would step on the innocent flames
we left in the grass before they spread out like TV waves
across the fields. I would like to mention also
how, later, I find myself, 1957, an altar boy
surrounded by church gold, the candles blazing

loudly, assisting the priest at the funeral of five children,
terrified at the five caskets in the aisle, white as sea shells,
terrified at the heavy scent of the altar flowers. It is the terror
of my own secret sin I would like finally to acknowledge.
But at this point I do not want to leave out
the small tragedies of my life hunched over the table of misery
with their oranges, eating the little wedges of fate.
They are whispering about a conspiratorial sunrise.
They are suspicious of Pythagoras, leaning back
against the piano, resting his elbows at an impossible angle.
Their own fears are fingering their way up through the embers.
I think it is myself I pray for, as much as Kevin who,
after setting small fires with me, must go home,
set the innocent fire that begins thirty feet from his house,
must forget some small spark crouching in the grass
only to have its brief whisper build into his own scream,
only to complete its story for him and his four sisters.
I'm sorry it is a story I must acknowledge for in this version
the sun is gone, there isn't enough moonlight to replace it,
no stars to touch the earth, no song to console me,
no story to hold off the truth, no Gypsy etching
that leads to another place, no way to switch channels,
some cowboy rescuing this night that has been leaning
on crutches, where the matches just seem to sleep
in our hands, a story so innocent or believable
that no dream, no terror, no guilt, nothing at all,
no flame of earth, could ever abandon or destroy,
and so I leave you this instead, the truth, all there is.